Portrait of a

What are the skills necessary for all students to become informed, active, engaged, and enthusiastic citizens in this rapidly-changing, increasingly diverse, interconnected society?

This book provides the framework to answer this question. Step by step, the book introduces a series of core competencies and skills that every student should acquire by the time they graduate. Then it provides useful, practical ways to implement these skills in classrooms. In this book, readers are given the tools to move beyond theory and into "action civics," empowering students to:

- Connect "textbook" civics to present-day challenges.
- Evaluate local issues and brainstorm collaborative solutions.
- Develop critical analysis skills to navigate misinformation.
- Engage in respectful, civil discourse on complex and even controversial topics.
- Forge intergenerational connections by working directly with their communities.

This timely and vital resource empowers educators to reclaim civics education and provide an open door for all students, regardless of their background or perspective. It's a roadmap for transforming our graduates into the active, engaged citizens our communities and our nation so desperately need.

The book is a professional learning tool, a curriculum guide, and a call to action all in one, making it the ideal resource for in-service social studies teachers and school leaders.

Darcy Daniels is an award-winning history educator with over two decades of experience teaching all levels from 5th grade through college, in the United States and abroad. She is a James Madison Memorial Fellow and the 2024 Massachusetts History Teacher of the Year.

Denise Furlong is assistant professor of education and director of Advanced Programs in Multilingual and Literacy Education at Georgian Court University in New Jersey. She is the co-author of *Learners First: Purpose and Practicality in Your Early Years of Teaching* (2025). She has over 25 years of experience teaching multilingual learners in New Jersey public schools ranging grades K–12.

Also Available from Routledge Eye On Education

(www.routledge.com/eyeoneducation)

Teaching Women's History: Breaking Barriers and Undoing Male Centrism in K-12 Social Studies
Kelsie Brook Eckert

Teaching LGBTQ+ History in High Schools: Practical Strategies and Voices of Experience
Stacie Brensilver Berman & Robert Cohen

Teaching Media Literacy with Social Media News: Practical Techniques for Middle and High School Classrooms
Roy S. Whitehurst

Teaching for CHANGE in the ELA Classroom: Integrating Social Justice and Critical Literacy for Grades 9–12
Dan Stockwell

Integrating Inquiry in Social Studies Classrooms
Carolyn Weber and Heather Hagan

The Antiracist English Language Arts Classroom
Keisha Rembert

Pop Culture Literacies: Teaching Interpretation, Response, and Composition in a Digital World
Mia Hood

Portrait of a Citizen

Strategies and Tools for Teaching Action Civics in Grades 6–12

Darcy Daniels and Denise Furlong

Routledge
Taylor & Francis Group
NEW YORK AND LONDON

Designed cover image: Getty Images

First published 2027
by Routledge
605 Third Avenue, New York, NY 10158

and by Routledge
4 Park Square, Milton Park, Abingdon, Oxon, OX14 4RN

Routledge is an imprint of the Taylor & Francis Group, an informa business

Library of Congress Cataloging-in-Publication Data
Names: Daniels, Darcy author | Furlong, Denise author
Title: Portrait of a citizen : strategies and tools for teaching action civics in grades 6-12 / Darcy Daniels and Denise M. Furlong.
Description: New York, NY : Routledge, 2027. | Series: Eye on education | Includes bibliographical references.
Identifiers: LCCN 2026012959 (print) | LCCN 2026012960 (ebook) | ISBN 9781041254171 hardback | ISBN 9781041255291 paperback | ISBN 9781003746614 ebook
Subjects: LCSH: Civics--Study and teaching (Middle school) | Civics--Study and teaching (Secondary) | Social sciences--Study and teaching (Middle school) | Social sciences--Study and teaching (Secondary) | Active learning
Classification: LCC LC1091 .D24 2027 (print) | LCC LC1091 (ebook)
LC record available at https://lccn.loc.gov/2026012959
LC ebook record available at https://lccn.loc.gov/2026012960

ISBN: 978-1-041-25417-1 (hbk)
ISBN: 978-1-041-25529-1 (pbk)
ISBN: 978-1-003-74661-4 (ebk)

DOI: 10.4324/9781003746614

Typeset in Palatino
by SPi Technologies India Pvt Ltd (Straive)

This book is dedicated to Mr. Bill Kennedy. Mr. Kennedy, *the sphere of influence is in direct proportion to the proximity thereof*. The influence of a great teacher continues long after all parties have left the classroom. Thank you for your guidance and the differences you have made for us and all your students.

Contents

Meet the Authors

Darcy

For Darcy Daniels, teaching is a family calling. As a third-generation educator, Darcy grew up understanding that the best lessons happen when students see themselves as part of a larger story. Over the past twenty years, her journey has taken her from the elementary classrooms of Paterson, New Jersey, to international schools in Budapest and college lecture halls across Massachusetts. Throughout these diverse experiences, her goal has remained the same: to move civics off the whiteboard and into the hands of the students.

Darcy currently serves as a Social Studies teacher and Instructional Partner at Nipmuc Regional High School in Massachusetts. She is a practitioner who believes in" learning by doing,"whether she is guiding AP students through the nuances of the Constitution or helping history students launch their first action civics project. Her commitment to authentic, student-led learning has earned her several prestigious honors, including being named the 2024 Massachusetts History Teacher of the Year and receiving a James Madison Memorial Fellowship.

A lifelong student of history and government, Darcy holds an MA in History from Monmouth University and a BA from Gettysburg College. When she isn't in the classroom or mentoring fellow teachers, she is often found giving tours of the Freedom Trail in Boston with Hub Town Tours. She lives and works in Massachusetts, where she remains dedicated to helping the next generation find their voices as active, engaged citizens.

Denise

Dr. Denise Furlong is an educator, advocate, and award-winning author whose work has made an impact in the world of educating learners with diverse needs. After over 25 years of teaching and mentoring in public schools in New Jersey (ranging grades K-12), Denise now works her dream job as an assistant professor of education at Georgian Court University in Lakewood, NJ. She also serves the university as the director of Advanced Programs for Multilingual and Literacy Education and finds an immense amount of joy in learning alongside both her graduate students and the student teachers she supervises.

Denise's first book, *Voices of Newcomers: Experiences of Multilingual Learners,* was the 2023 recipient of the Delta Kappa Gamma International Educator Book Award and is a popular "go-to" professional book study choice for educators. She also co-authored a bilingual children's book, *Ben and the Amazing Animal Adventure,* which was honored with the M. Jerry Weiss Award for Children's Literature. Her 2025 collaboration with Dr. Keri Orange-Jones, *Learners First: Purpose and Practicality in Your Early Years of Teaching,* has become a solid staple in new teacher mentorship and university programs as a holistic and authentic way to support our newest colleagues. She feels strongly that it is the responsibility of all stakeholders to build the foundation for the teachers and students who come after us.

A proud alumna of The College of New Jersey and the Rutgers Graduate School of Education, Denise recently was honored with the 2025 Distinguished Service Award from the GSE Alumni Association. She is active in DKG International, NJTESOL/NJBE, and is also involved in working for the National Education Association at the national level as a proud union member.

Denise has participated in educational conferences as keynote or featured speaker around the world and recently presented on her fourth continent! She loves to travel and learn about education and culture in other countries and looks forward to new and different opportunities both in the United States and abroad.

Denise is a proud wife and mom who lives at the Jersey Shore.

Darcy & Denise together

We are high-school friends who sat together in AP US History I & II. Life has taken us in different directions and through unique paths, but we stayed in touch and followed one another's ups and downs over the years. We never forgot the ways we learned about history and civics in Mr. Kennedy's class at Brick Township High School. (Go Dragons!)

Darcy's experiences as a social studies educator brought up the topic that we all were wondering: How do we engage young people meaningfully in civics and local government? These conversations are how the idea for this book came to light. We believe that educators want to know how to build confidence, knowledge, and interest in our government within our future leaders. And our future leaders want to be empowered through their unique voices and experiences.

According to Denise, Darcy is one of those people who brings out the best in people. She is a kind listener with a generous heart who makes people smile wherever she goes. According to Darcy, Denise is the greatest cheerleader a friend can have.

Acknowledgements

Darcy

Thanks to my mom and dad, Margo and Tony Daniels, who were my first teachers.

To Michael, I'm so lucky to have married you.

To Wendy and Penny, I'm proud, every single day, to be your mom.

Denise, I am thrilled with this collaboration, thank you for everything.

Bill, Sarah, Evora, Travis, Amy, Yully, Chris, Linden, Susie, Kelly, David and Kim, thank you for your unwavering support and well-timed humor.

Matt, Dan, Brian, Chrissy, Kathy, Tara, Kerry and JJ: I learn from you daily and I'm lucky to call you my colleagues.

Brad, thank you for the many discussions on democracy.

Mary Anne, John, Maureen and Cheryl, thank you for the inspiration and the guidance.

To my fellow tour guides at Hub Town Tours, Huzzah for the Republic!

To my students, don't stop until you're proud. You are the future.

Denise

Thank you to the best support system I could have: my family and my friends who are my chosen family. You relentlessly show up for me and remind me who I am (I am my parents' daughter, Tim's wife, and my kids' mom!) when I doubt myself.

Darcy, it has been such a joy to learn from you. Thank you for taking me on this journey with you!

Tim, Ryan, Joey, & Sarah: I love you and I hope I make you proud. On to our next adventure!

Theresa & Bob, Matt, Kristen, AJ, Danny, Alaina, Karen, Sue, Jennifer: Thanks for always showing up, no questions asked.

To the educators who shared their voices with us: You are incredibly appreciated and we value you immensely!

Keri, Carly, Dorina, Carol, Deb, Gill, Veronica: I so appreciate my teacher squad and you are all incredibly important to me. Women who support others without reservation or competition are the best citizens of all.

To all my students (past, present, future): Your voice is valuable and your impact on the world is incredible. Thank you for being YOU and thank you for teaching me.

Darcy and Denise

Thanks to Colleen Gormley, Mark Pappas and Brian Rainville for being our first readers.

Thanks to Josh King, for all the help with the photos.

Thanks to Paul Gorski for seeing this book's potential.

Thanks to Megha Patel, Jessica Sawin and the staff at Taylor & Francis.

1

The Problem

The Crisis at the Core of Democracy

As educators, we all share a vision: students leaving our classrooms prepared to be active, informed, and empathetic participants in their communities and our democracy. But achieving that vision often feels nearly unreachable. This lofty goal is blocked by deep, overlapping obstacles rooted in educational pitfalls, underfunding, societal divisions, and growing intergenerational disconnection. The neglect is starting to become obvious to those who are paying attention.

According to the CIRCLE Post-2024 Election Poll from Tufts University, young people (ages 18–29) are feeling increasingly disconnected with national politics. Of the respondents to the poll, only 24% of young people said they felt like they are a part of a group or movement in which people express themselves politically. (Medina et al., 2025.)

The Marginalization of Social Studies

At the school level, the teaching of social studies has progressively been marginalized in favor of other core subjects like reading, writing, math, and science due to the emphasis on high-stakes testing. These high-stakes tests are the benchmark for governing

DOI: 10.4324/9781003746614-1

bodies to hold schools accountable. Teachers, therefore, focus on the subjects that are tested. As a result, social studies is left to the last minute, or when there's some spare time. Ask any elementary teacher how much time they can devote to social studies, and they'll likely respond with a laugh, followed by "not much." One study shows that elementary school teachers spend three hours every week on social studies while spending 11 hours per week on English Language Arts (ELA) (Fitchett et al., 2014.) This limited allocation of time means that social studies often becomes the default period for interruptions—fire drills, annual nurse check-ups, or school-wide assemblies. Consequently, the reduced time for social studies instruction translates into even less time for effective professional development, leaving teachers feeling decreasingly confident in their ability to teach the subject effectively (Ahlgrim-Delzell et al., 2022) After all, social studies is big! It includes maps and geography, history, civics, economics, religion, politics, philosophy, and more. It is also skills-based rather than knowledge-based, and many elementary teachers feel more comfortable teaching knowledge than developing skills in their students. Ultimately, it's a withering of subject knowledge on the part of general education teachers that creates a self-perpetuating cycle of less time being devoted to social studies.

That means, functionally, that students are only learning about history and civics in their middle school and high school years. We have effectively cut out six years of learning. So when we teach about crucial topics connected to citizenship, it's to a population of students who likely have not been introduced to it before. That puts us at a disadvantage from the get-go. Likewise, civics is not funded properly. While the federal government spends roughly 50 dollars per student for STEM funding, the amount they spend per student on civics education is just 5 cents (Woodwell, 2024).

The inevitable outcome of this profound, structural neglect—in curriculum priority, teacher confidence, and funding—is a student body demonstrably unprepared for active and engaged citizenship. The statistics are alarming: The National Assessment of Educational Progress (NAEP) reported that only 22% of eighth-grade students were proficient in their civics test. This means that 78% of our emerging citizens lack the foundational knowledge required for informed democratic participation.

The Action Civics Gap

A significant contributing factor to this unpreparedness is that students don't feel connected to their communities due to the lack of "**action civics**." Far too often, civics classes scratch the surface, stopping at a theoretical understanding of the three branches of government, how a bill becomes a law, and the Bill of Rights. Students are rarely given the opportunity to interact directly with their communities, to evaluate local strengths and challenges, and then to collaboratively brainstorm and implement solutions. The curriculum often remains solely at the theoretical level, never progressing to the actual doing of civic engagement. Students don't get to try out their skills of civic engagement. In addition, with over-scheduled lives, students rarely benefit from intergenerational interactions. This gap used to be filled by students joining civic clubs or organizations, but participation in civic organizations has steadily gone downward for the last 50 years.

This isolation from their communities is detrimental; it prevents students from feeling connected to their surroundings and from forging vital intergenerational connections. Yet, the community equally stands to gain from witnessing and harnessing the creativity, teamwork, and ingenuity of its youth. After all, in most communities, the school in town is the largest collection of people, with the most creativity, cooperation, and energy of anywhere in the area. Don't believe us? Go into a fourth-grade classroom on Valentine's Day and you'll see that you could possibly power a whole community with the energy with the students that day.

The Social and Media Divides

Beyond the four walls of their schools, students already are interconnected with people around the world through social media, but they are also immersed in an increasingly divisive political climate. Many Americans now rely on a single news source, leading to insulated echo chambers that reinforce confirmation bias (Kelly, 2021). We are living in a nation of "silos," where compromise is frequently perceived as a weakness. This environment is further complicated by rampant misinformation circulating unchecked on social media. According to Pew Research, over half of Americans (54%) now get their news from social media either "sometimes" or "often."

Even more challenging is the tsunami of artificial intelligence, which generates content that students (and many of us) cannot tell if it's real or not. Re-teaching skepticism is going to become a critical step in political awareness. Though not new, Edgar Allen Poe said, "Believe nothing you hear and only half of what you see" in 1845. Now there are entire apps dedicated to creating false video clips. It is an unmooring of understanding between what is real and what is created.

We are taught to beware of easy answers to complex problems, but they are just that, *easy*. Given this landscape, where do students find the opportunity to truly grapple with complex issues, understand how government functions, and discover how to constructively contribute to their communities and nation? Teachers are increasingly apprehensive about introducing controversial issues in class, leading to a noticeable atrophy in classroom deliberations. They fear losing their jobs, and, consequently, decide to avoid these topics altogether. A recent survey showed that 56% of teachers surveyed don't discuss potentially controversial topics, such as ethnicity or race, politics, slavery, gender, religion, sexual orientation, the Holocaust, or sex education, in the classroom (Ujifusa & Harwin, 2022).

The question remains: *If we, as educators, shy away from these crucial conversations, where else will students learn about them and practice discussing them in a safe, guided environment?* It must be schools. In many ways, schools are the last refuge of critical analysis, civil discourse, and celebrating differences.

Educators already do so many good things. The challenge, then, is to transfer the excellent work we are already doing, add to it, and take our graduates and turn them into active and engaged citizens.

> By teaching our students about democracy they can go home to their communities and teach their family and friends about the ideas and topics we are learning about. This helps the community because often families in our community do not bother to vote in local elections because they typically do not know who the candidates are, or how these elections really matter for their individual communities.
>
> —Marie, history teacher

The Portrait of a Citizen Framework

Portrait of a Citizen: Fostering Equity and Engagement in Action Civics in Grades 6–12 is a direct response to this crisis. We worked backward from the ultimate goal, asking the central question:

What are the skills necessary for all students in this rapidly changing, increasingly diverse, interconnected society, to become informed, active, engaged, and enthusiastic citizens in the United States?

The answer is our blueprint: The Portrait of a Citizen Matrix.

It is tempting to view civic education solely through the lens of content: historical facts, governmental structures, and founding documents. Yet, we must recognize that effective citizenship is not merely about knowing the facts, but about mastering the skills to apply them. This is the crucial shift: moving from a focus on rote memorization to developing transferable skills—like analyzing bias, ethical problem-solving, and collaborative consensus-building—that students will use in college, career, and community life.

The Matrix achieves this critical outcome through two essential design elements. First, the Matrix is constructed with stackable skills. Each of the six core competencies is broken down into specific "I Can" statements that are designed for vertical alignment from sixth through grade twelve. This means a student's competency is built year-over-year, preventing instruction from being repetitive and ensuring a clear, measurable progression toward mastery. Second, by explicitly naming these competencies, we provide the essential common language necessary for all departments and grade levels to collaborate on this vital work.

To address this, we defined six Core Competencies essential for an informed, active, and enthusiastic citizen:

1. **Civic Knowledge:** Understanding governmental structures, components, rights, and responsibilities.
2. **Community Engagement:** Being connected to local strengths and challenges, and willing to take action to effect positive change.
3. **Ethical Decision-Making:** Grasping the values, ethics, and processes that guide professional and civic leaders.
4. **Critical Thinking:** Navigating complex information, being skeptical of propaganda, and providing evidence for one's actions.
5. **National and Global Awareness:** Recognizing the forces and bodies that guide daily life in the national and international spheres.
6. **Differences Celebrated:** Respecting varied lived experiences and perspectives, recognizing that differences strengthen the nation.

This model draws on a structure already familiar to thousands of educators—the "Portrait of a Learner" or "Portrait of a Graduate" framework—but focuses it entirely on civic capacity. This structure has been adopted by thousands of schools in all fifty states. It lays out the goal, and then subsequent chapters explain each competency and skill. The Matrix provides a clear path for professional development, curriculum alignment, and assessment. It aligns with the C3 (College, Career, and Civic Life) framework laid out by the National Council of Social Studies (NCSS) in an easy-to-digest format, ensuring its relevance in any classroom nationwide.

What You Will Find in This Book

This book breaks down the complex concept of citizenship into six core, measurable competencies. These are the skill sets every student must acquire or master by the time they graduate high school to be effective citizens.

We introduce these competencies through a practical lens, moving beyond abstract concepts and into "action civics," empowering students to:

- Connect "textbook" civics to present-day challenges.
- Develop critical analysis skills to navigate misinformation.
- Engage in respectful, civil discourse on complex and even controversial topics.
- Forge connections by working directly with their communities.

In the chapters that follow, we will guide you through:

- **The Foundations (Chapters 2–3):** We address the sticky term of "citizen" and introduce the six-competency Matrix (Civic Knowledge, Community Engagement, Ethical Decision-Making, Critical Thinking, National and Global Awareness, and Differences Celebrated).
- **The Competencies (Chapters 4–9):** We dedicate a full chapter to each of the six competencies, providing specific, actionable "I Can" statements and a host of exercises, resources, and vignettes from the field. Each chapter also includes dedicated sections on BEST Practices to ensure equity and access for students with learning challenges, multilingual learners, and gifted students.
- **Implementation (Chapter 10):** We explain how to integrate the Matrix into your existing curriculum, department, or district, and offer guidance on how to customize or make your own matrix to meet the unique ethos of your school community.

We seek to move beyond theory and provide the tools necessary to truly empower every student—regardless of their background, nation of origin, or learning roadblock—to understand their rights and responsibilities. Further, as we consider different ways to engage learners, including students with learning challenges, multilingual newcomers, and those in need of trauma-informed Social Emotional Learning (SEL), each section of this book is driven by how to best provide access to all. Civics must be an open door for everyone in our schools with respectful discourse and accessible engagement. This commitment is codified in our BEST Practices framework which stands for Bridging, Extension, Support, and Teamwork.

This book is a timely and vital resource for educators, administrators, and curriculum specialists. It is not just a curriculum guide; it is a roadmap for transforming our graduates into the active, engaged citizens whom our communities and our nation so desperately need. We hope you'll find it to be the lens through which you look at your lessons when you are planning to make the most of every lesson.

During a 10-day tour of World War and Holocaust sites in Belgium, Germany, and France, my group traveled on the Munich underground on our way to Dachau Concentration Camp. Our tour guide was sharing details in English about Bavaria and the history of Dachau when, during a pause, a German woman asked him in her language what we were doing. After he explained that we had come to learn about the history and tragedies of the place, she turned to us and said in English, "I am so glad that we are still sharing our history, and that you came so far to be a part of learning from the past so it never happens again." I will never forget those words. She could have looked away or minimized the past, but instead she affirmed the importance of remembering—even the darkest parts of history—so that we can learn, grow, and avoid repeating the same mistakes.

—Kaitlyn, adjunct history professor

References

Ahlgrim-Delzell, L., Clark, R., Heafner, T., & Fitchett, P. (2022). Assessing elementary teacher professional development and confidence in teaching social studies (ED656051). *ERIC*. https://files.eric.ed.gov/fulltext/ED656051.pdf

Fitchett, P. G., Heafner, T. L., & VanFossen, P. (2014). An analysis of time prioritization for social studies in elementary school classrooms. *Journal of Curriculum and Instruction*, 8(2), 7–35. https://www.joci.ecu.edu/index.php/JoCI/article/view/343

Kelly, M. (2021, December 9). *Political polarization and its echo chambers: Surprising new, cross-disciplinary perspectives from Princeton*. Princeton University. https://www.princeton.edu/news/2021/12/09/political-polarization-and-its-echo-chambers-surprising-new-cross-disciplinary

Medina, A., Siegel-Stechler, K., & Suzuki, S. (2025, January 15). Young people and the 2024 election: Struggling, disconnected, and dissatisfied. *CIRCLE (Center for Information & Research on Civic Learning and Engagement)*. https://circle.tufts.edu/latest-research/2024-poll-barriers-issues-economy

Ujifusa, A., & Harwin, J. (2022, October 13). How cultural and political issues resonate with K-12 educators in charts. *Education Week*. https://www.edweek.org/policy-politics/how-cultural-and-political-issues-resonate-with-k-12-educators-in-charts/2022/10

Woodwell, W. (2024). Connecting civic education and a healthy democracy. *Carnegie Corporation of New York*. https://www.carnegie.org/our-work/article/healthy-democracies-need-to-invest-in-civic-education-heres-how-states-can-help/

2

The Sticky Term

Citizen

Introduction

There are certain words connected to the teaching of civics that hold emotional connotations. Few would deny that the term citizen carries meaning that is strongly felt to be the warp and weft of the fabric of our country. Much of the current discussion surrounding this term refers to the documentation connected to a human's legal status in a country. On balance, citizenship can also be viewed as a term that separates groups of people into categories that may go well beyond place of birth or documents they may hold.

If we are considering the term *citizen* as a person who has legally recognized rights to a country or state by birth or by naturalization process, then is being a good citizen something that not all people can do? Webster Dictionary also identifies a citizen as being an inhabitant of a particular area. While this is more in line with an inclusive view of civics, there is often a black-and-white view of the concept of citizenship. These views may represent non-citizens as people who are the enemy of citizens or may be filled with misinformation or partial truths.

This chapter explores these views of citizenship and how we as educators navigate the balance between ensuring that we

DOI: 10.4324/9781003746614-2

provide a safe space for all humans in our educational settings and allowing our students to work through tough topics in which there may be disagreements. As educators, we acknowledge and appreciate that our students come from different backgrounds and have varied life stories. This is the beauty of our schools; we learn alongside others who bring an incredible diversity to our space. Not everyone is going to agree with different views on action civics—and that is OK. Creating a space in which human rights are respected, voices are heard (even if we don't agree), and people are open to learning from one another provides the space in which we all can grow.

As citizenship is an area in which there are strong opinions, we intentionally set this chapter up in a way that we can take this journey with our readers. There is constant reflection on the use of language and how it represents both us and our students. We may have our own views and opinions about certain groups of people (in this case, possibly undocumented people) and we recognize that our students—or their families—may identify as a member of one of these groups. In order for our students to all feel safe and have a sense of belonging, we must ensure that we communicate that to them—no matter what their situation may be outside the classroom.

> I have a unit on citizenship and we discuss how to gain it but also how to lose it. We have a lot of kids whose citizenship is questionable so it's a tough unit. The kids know not to say anything nasty to another kid or I will respond accordingly. I can't tolerate cruelty.
>
> —Christy, 7th grade social studies teacher

When we first sat down to discuss this book, we initially said that this book will be neutral in terms of politics and they won't be addressed. We then reflected. Education is inherently political. Civics education is engaging in the political arena of education while processing and understanding the ways that we participate in our government, community, and society. So, while we certainly do not write this book through a lens of specific parties, we espouse the ideals of diversity, voice, inclusion, and equity. As sticky of a term that *citizen* is, we want to have open and honest discourse about how teachers can engage with their students through these ideals.

> **Time to reflect:** *When we teach about being a good citizen or citizenship, are we referring to the politics of documentation or the character of being a good person? Do we teach a delineation of these concepts and (if yes) under which circumstances?*

Key Vocabulary from Merriam-Webster

Citizen: a person with allegiance or pertinence to a particular country or place by nature of birth or naturalization

Birthright citizenship: the notion that being born in the United States or in one of its territories grants one citizenship status

Naturalization: the process through which a foreign-born person becomes a citizen of a country, state, or kingdom, usually after fulfilling specific legal requirements such as residency, passing civics and language tests, and swearing an oath of allegiance

Culturally responsive pedagogy: intentional ways that teachers are sensitive to the diverse perspectives, learning strengths, and languaging of their students

Refugee: a person who is forced to leave their country because of war, persecution, natural disaster, or other dangers

The Complex History of U.S. Citizenship

Citizenship and civic engagement have always had a complex, and sometimes separate, relationship throughout U.S. history. Before the United States was formed, the American colonists already practiced fundamental principles of civic engagement, even without the full rights of British citizenship. They exercised their right to a free and fair trial, the right to peaceably assemble, the right to petition the government, and the right to freedom of speech. Colonists also used boycotts as a powerful form of protest. The founding generation, themselves without representation in the British Parliament that legislated for them, showed their displeasure through assembly, boycotts, petitions, and legal action. This period of conflict, which began nearly twenty years before the Revolutionary War, culminated in eight years of armed conflict before the United States of America was born as thirteen independent states.

Beadie et al. (2021) discuss the history of the word *citizenship* in terms of the history of the United States and connect it to the notions of *those in power* and the *powerless*. DiSalvo (2022) maintains that traditional ideals concerning citizenship were "exclusionary and exercised to reproduce dominant ideologies" (p. 21). The concept of being a citizen today is just as nuanced and complex as it has been over the years: Is it a line in the sand to separate the rights of people or is it a positive term that is inclusive?

For some, citizenship may be the line between the "haves" and the "have nots" when considering documentation and status. The process of becoming a citizen in the United States is a thorough and detailed one and may take several years to complete. Bauml and colleagues (Bauml et al., 2021) maintain that the singular view of citizenship that is portrayed in many civics courses may turn some students off from the idea that they are part of the democratic process. In other words, if they do not see themselves represented in the concept presented of citizenship, they may feel that they do not have a space in society or a voice in the government (Dejaeghere, 2013; Malin, 2011, as noted by Bauml et al., 2021).

When a group of men gathered in Philadelphia to create a more just government, they did so with a new hope of including the voices of those who were previously unheard: white, landowning men. However, they failed to extend this new project of liberty, equality, and justice to others. Despite Abigail Adams's famous plea to her husband John to "remember the ladies" while drafting the new laws, the Constitution did not grant women citizenship rights. While the Constitution offered new hope to the world, it remained an incomplete dream for many. Even though women and African Americans were not considered citizens at the time, they were still expected to engage in the government and were active participants in shaping the nation's path forward, often through challenging the status quo.

When John Adams wrote the Massachusetts Constitution, for example, he wrote that all men were "born free and equal." It was an enslaved woman named Mum Bett who heard that and approached a lawyer to help her sue for her freedom, along with a man named Brom. Simultaneously a man named Quock Walker also sued. It was determined that they had a case and won their freedom. Soon afterward, Massachusetts outlawed slavery, and by the time the 1790 census rolled around, there were no more enslaved workers in the Commonwealth of Massachusetts.

Other enslaved workers sued for their freedom throughout the decades. It wasn't until the case of *Dred Scott* v. *Sanford* (1856) that Chief Justice Roger Taney stated that black people had no rights of citizens whatsoever, but that was sixty-five years after Mum Bett first sued for her freedom. It took a Civil War and the Fourteenth Amendment (ratified in 1868) to change that course.

It took another thirty years for a challenge to the idea of birthright citizenship through the Supreme Court case of *US* v. *Wong Kim Ark*, which applied the principle originally thought to mean just those who were enslaved, to all babies born in the United States, excepting Native Americans.

Native Americans had their own obstacles, independent of other minority groups, because they were first seen as independent nationals, then dependent nationals, and then finally as American citizens. They did not get the right to vote in the United States until 1924, with the passing of the Indian Citizenship Act.

These minority groups still see continued struggles to reach parity in the realm of civic equality. The Voting Rights Act of 1965 helped to foster increased equality, in large part to the visibility of the Civil Rights Movement, championed by many who did not yet have the right to vote, teenagers. Those brave children used the power of petition and assembly, largely in a nonviolent way, to make their voices heard. Think of the students at the Woolworth lunch counter or those who were freedom riders. Many of those people did not have the right to vote yet simply because they were too young to do so, and complicated by the fact that they were a racial minority.

> The word "citizen" is a sticky one because it carries both rights and responsibilities, but also histories of exclusion. One story that often illustrates this tension is the experience of Japanese Americans during World War II: even though many were U.S. citizens by birth, they were still forced into internment camps because of suspicion and prejudice. Their citizenship did not fully protect them, which raises questions about who gets to belong and under what conditions. On a more hopeful note, stories of the Civil Rights Movement highlight how individuals—sometimes denied the full recognition of citizenship—used language, protest, and collective action to expand its meaning. For example, Fannie Lou Hamer famously declared, 'Nobody's free until everybody's free,' showing how the word citizen can become not just a legal category, but a moral call to ensure equity and participation for all. Adding reflections like these can help students see that citizenship is not just a status on paper, but an evolving practice of belonging, responsibility, and recognition.
>
> —Kaitlyn, adjunct professor

Citizenship and Democracy

Democracy is the cornerstone of our collective beliefs as a country in the United States. Many citizens feel it is one of the things that set us apart as a free country and a reason why the United States is a nation in which people have rights and freedoms.

However, in many instances, civil rights in the United States extend much beyond the concept of citizenship, illustrating the need to protect the lives of all humans. While citizenship can be a factor in some rights, such as the right to vote, it has been demonstrated in multiple Supreme Court decisions that you do not need to be a citizen to enjoy the same civil rights, like the right to due process. For example, while the majority decision in *Gideon v. Wainwright* (1963) does not specifically use the term "non-citizen" it instead refers to the term "any person" or "the accused," because the decision rests upon the Fourteenth Amendment (which uses the term "any person") and the Sixth Amendment (which uses the term "accused") in all court cases. Perhaps the most illustrative passage states,

> The right of one charged with crime to counsel may not be deemed fundamental and essential to fair trials in some countries, but it is in ours. From the very beginning, our state and national constitutions and laws have laid great emphasis on procedural and substantive safeguards designed to assure fair trials before impartial tribunals in which every defendant stands equal before the law.

This legal evolution challenges the traditional view that being a "good citizen" simply means following the rules. Westheimer and Ladson-Billings (2024) likened a typical view of good citizenship to solid moral character and following the rules. However, we teach critical thinking as a core skill across the curriculum. Are good citizens not supposed to question authority, or are they obligated to follow the rules if they determine that they are not ethical or morally in line with one's values? If one is truly examining laws or events through a critical lens and speaking out for what they believe to be the better good, is their standing as a "good citizen" at risk? Westheimer and Ladsen-Billings also maintained that indoctrination in schools under the guise of citizenship has been used in some of the worst atrocities in history (Westheimer & Ladson-Billings, 2024). There is a disconnect between what may have historically been considered good citizenship and the deep questioning and critical thinking skills that we know are necessary for our students to deeply learn about a topic.

> I met with my local senator and I asked him about how he personally was advocating for our schools. When I told him that I taught multilingual learners for many years, he then made a comment about "illegals" [referencing a group of people] and how one of the things he supports changing in public schools is to deport all of them.
>
> —Denise

Citizenship and Documentation

The notion of documentation to demonstrate citizenship status is not a new one, nor is it necessarily a negative thing. Documentation is important for travel, voting, and other services that are available for citizens and is standard practice in many countries. There are many notions regarding documentation that may be only partially understood by many people in the United States and we seek to explore some of them here in a place of learning and positive discourse.

There are some very common responses to the notion of humans without documentation living in our communities.

> "They should go through the process and just become citizens!"
> "My family went about it the right way when they came to this country; so should these people."
> "They are here just not paying taxes and not contributing to our country."
> "They should go back where they came from."
> "They are breaking the law and are bad people."

The rhetoric around documentation in the current political climate is polarizing for many and potentially confusing for others. As citizens, we often do not understand the processes and guidelines for citizenship and it is important that educators have a baseline comprehension of the different facets.

SEL connection: This may be a difficult topic for some of your students or families for a variety of reasons. Understanding that there are different backgrounds and perspectives among the students in your class—all of which are valid, lived experiences—is key to a culturally responsive classroom. Focus on listening and learning.

The Question of Being a United States Citizen

According to the United States Citizenship and Immigration Services (n.d.-a), there are ten steps to becoming a naturalized citizen. These steps range from determining if you are eligible to apply for citizenship to taking civics and English assessments to background checks. In order to begin to see if a person is eligible for this process, one must lawfully live in the United States for a number of years, either by having a green card (a Permanent Resident card) or through marriage to a citizen before the application is begun. From there, the processing time is estimated by the government to be 8–14 months.

While this sounds reasonable, there are some challenges in this system for many people. The process for obtaining a green card is often lengthy (listed as 7 months to several years) and this must be issued at least 5 years before one can begin the application for naturalization. Also, only certain groups of people are eligible to apply for a green card—which disqualifies many immigrants based on country of origin or other factors (U.S. Citizenship and Immigration Services, n.d.-b) So, there are some immigrants who may never qualify for an application for a green card nor citizenship under these current guidelines.

Some people may enter the United States through applications for refugee status and this is another way that they may have some documentation as they settle here. These people come from a country in which they are in such danger that they are forced to leave and seek shelter in another country. The United

States views these applications on a case-by-case basis and—even if they are accepted as refugees—their status can be revoked at any time (as has been the case for several protected groups in 2025).

These processes change over time—sometimes with different political administrations and other times with changes in relations with different countries. When people say, "My family did it the right way!," this may or may not have been something that was easier to attain in that time period. In even the best of circumstances (and with good, hardworking people) now, there may be no pathway for them to do the "right" thing or they may be living here illegally while they work on this process.

> I had my 8th graders (US Hist since 1860) do a project on government structures before we studied the USSR, Mao's China, and other communist countries. Each group was given a situation prompt (a war just ended, a famine just ended, there is a threat of nuclear attack, etc.) and had to create a society in response to the situation. Groups chose how they wanted to explain their societies and most groups chose through a board game that allows players to experience what life is like in the society or as a series of journal entries from people of different experiences living in the community. It is amazing how quickly they disregard any concept of citizen rights and decide the "best" option for everyone in the society. In discussing the projects after they were complete, it was interesting to see that the creators of each project were very confident that they had designed the ideal society and their classmates all suggested different aspects that they saw as unfair or as a government overreach. This led to an interesting conversation about who has rights in a society and when those rights might be expanded or restricted.
>
> —Paige, teacher librarian

Why Would People Want to Move to Another Country Illegally?

This is a valid question that many people ask, and the reasons may be as unique as each human is. As a society we value following the law and see it as one of the ways we keep order; it is often difficult to see situations in which perhaps we perceive that others may appear to not value this as much as we do. It appears to many to be a black-and-white issue: Either something is legal or it is not. While we can acknowledge that this point of view comes from a lens of privilege in that this is not something that we have had to experience, we also may be able to acknowledge that these situations may fall in the "grey" area in which there may not be a clear delineation between right and wrong.

We consider how challenging such a journey may be and wonder why someone would choose to do this or subject their family to such potential danger. When one's family is in danger or is being physically harmed, is it acceptable to do whatever may be necessary to save them? When one cannot put food on the table and children are starving in the current situation, is that a reason why one may flee? If one lives in a war zone or in areas where gangs are taking over the schools and leaving may be the only way one survives, is there empathy for that situation? While these may not be the reasons why everyone leaves their home to cross a border, many immigrants may have similar stories.

People may also have misinformation about the rules/laws about immigration to other countries. They may think that they have a potential pathway to citizenship that they can easily complete and then build their lives. They may also think that there are ways that they can support their family in ways that were not accessible in their home country. They may find safe places in which their children will have a better chance at a fulfilling life. While this may be difficult for some to believe, the ways that people may get information about other countries may not be reliable.

The landmark case *Plyler* v. *Doe* (1982) determined that schools were not permitted to inquire about the citizenship status of students and that all students were entitled to an education with or without a social security number or other identifying information. Until this point, schools were permitted to deny an education to families who could not provide documentation of citizenship. While this ruling has not yet been officially overturned by the Trump administration, as of this writing there has been much discourse about the rights of undocumented students in schools and if they are legally entitled to be there.

Citizenship and Civics Education

"Civic education is itself political. The fact that it implies citizenship means that it has always been embedded in conflicts over who should be accorded the status of citizens and recognized as having civil and political rights" (Beadie et al., 2021, p. 112). As citizens are the focus of many declarations and documents in our government and in our societal norms, it is a natural next step that the concept of a citizen guides much of civics education. Following are some ideas to support discourse addressing this concept in class:

- The idea of being a citizen may be interchangeable with "inhabitant" or "resident" of a country or area. While this isn't the typical connotation for this word outside of a school setting currently, this may be specified as the use of this term in civics class. This would mitigate the concept that civics is only engagement for certain populations. *Why may this be a controversial take on this term in the current political climate?*
- There may be an aspirational view of becoming a citizen and this can be a goal for students who do not have documentation at this time. A goal for students who are already citizens with documentation may be to find ways to become more active in their citizenship. *Why may someone opt to pursue citizenship in the United States and why may one choose not to do so?*
- The notion of the rights and responsibilities of citizens can be discussed within the context of benefits and contributions. This may be considered alongside the responsibilities without the benefits for those who do not have

documentation. *Are there benefits that should be exclusively for documented citizens of a country? What ways can non-documented humans contribute to society?*

- People who were born in territories such as Puerto Rico are United States citizens, but Puerto Ricans have debated the pros and cons of becoming a state for decades. *What may be the benefits and downsides of statehood versus being a territory? What effect would this have on Puerto Rican citizens?*

Imperative to these conversations are the unique perspectives that all humans have. In our society today, it may be difficult to have respectful discourse when parties are in strong disagreement; this is essential to the civics educational space and must be something that is established immediately. We acknowledge and celebrate free speech—and we also ensure that the culture and climate of a classroom is safe for all students. While this may at times be challenging to manage, honest and kind discourse is necessary to learning and creates learners who are willing to take risks, stretch their thinking, and encourage others to do the same.

The notion of "curiosity" in seeking others' perspectives is a positive place to begin and an essential point to make. We as humans can ask questions from a place of respect that may help us truly understand why people make different decisions as long as the judgment is removed. *Why would someone enter a different country/space without going through the "proper" channels?* While this doesn't attack anyone or judge others' lives, this is an honest question that may teach about the varied life experiences of humans in the community or around the world. Being open to changing opinions and learning from one another is a valuable skill to model and teach—and acknowledging that sometimes agreeing to disagree respectfully is important as well.

Time to reflect: *If classroom conversations regarding citizenship take a turn that may make some students uncomfortable or feeling targeted, what may educators do to protect space for respectful discourse while ensuring that all students feel safe?*

We maintain that the notion of participation and voice is necessary to begin at a very young age and should not be "saved" until students are older. As students begin learning about "community helpers" and basic information about their towns or cities in early elementary school, they begin their work in very basic pre-civics discussions as young children. Topics shift and become more specific to the government as students advance. Many educators feel that students may not be ready for more in-depth knowledge about local, state, and federal government until they are much older. But it is never too early for students to see that there are different ways to approach the same problem, which in turn allows them to be more elastic with their own thinking. As they go through the grades, civics may be a small part of the social studies curriculum until they reach a point at which either they elect to take a civics course or it becomes a requirement for that grade or for graduation.

> When I taught the election cycle during last year's presidential election, I decided to have a snack election instead. The kids caucused for their party—salty or sweet. Then we held primaries. The entire school voted in our election after we postered the school and the kids had a lot of fun. They really got into the whole process. At no point did we discuss Trump or Harris. It was great.
>
> —Christy, civics educator

As mentioned in various parts of this book, it is critical to broaden the scope of the information that is available to our students that may give them perspective on their place in society. Our worlds have expanded to allow us to share space with those who are geographically or culturally in different areas. Primary sources may be readily available in real time that opens perspectives and pathways that may previously not have been accessible. With so much information at our fingertips, it is important to distinguish between "research" and propaganda or news presented in a way that doesn't present a balanced or full picture. It's quite easy for any of us to find data that fits our narrative and call it research but it is important to build our students' critical thinking skills through analysis of sources as well.

Digital citizenship is often defined as the responsible use of the internet and potentially etiquette surrounding interactions with others via online communication. We propose that this term also includes ways that we establish connections with others via technology and we learn about different cultures and places that would have historically been beyond our horizons. Engaging our students in digital citizenship broadens their scope of what it means to be a citizen, human, and contributing member of our global society. Truly understanding and embracing the notion of digital citizenship provides our students opportunities to experience the world outside their geographic and sociocultural space.

Educators must really go through the work of identifying and reflecting on their own perspectives and potential biases regarding their students and their places in our society. Action civics is just that: subscribing to the notion that we all have a voice and a responsibility to actively engage in our communities and society is crucial.

> Civic education opportunities for marginalized youth are minimal and often narrowly conceptualized, leaving those who most need empowerment the least opportunity to feel valued as citizens, learn important civic knowledge, and develop key values, skills, and dispositions related to citizenship.
>
> (Blevins, 2022, p. 2)

Culturally Responsive/Sustaining Pedagogy and Civics

As in all content areas, educators must consider their unique students when engaging them in learning. Access points, diverse perspectives, and different life experiences are all things that must be at the forefront of teaching and planning. Culturally responsive pedagogy means many things to educators, but with respect to civics and citizenship we maintain that there are five guidelines to consider. We also mention culturally sustaining pedagogy as this is being referenced more through the perspective that we want our students to maintain their cultures and we support them in their beautiful uniqueness and build on the strengths that they have.

Diversity is Our Strength: There is no language, class, or cultural hierarchy in which some are elevated above others. Inclusive of any documentation status, all students are welcomed and have a safe space in the school and classroom. *All ways that we are diverse are valuable parts of who we are and opportunities for the collective community to learn and grow.*

Keep it Civil: While our opinions are worthwhile and honest conversation is encouraged, hate speech or derogatory language are not tolerated. This may be a challenging concept for students depending on age and exposure to this type of discourse and this may be revisited many times over the course of the year. Let's face it; there is a lot of "dinnertable talk" about the state of immigration in the United States and children may repeat things that they have heard in other settings that may make others feel unsafe (Furlong, 2022). *We can have respectful conversations in which we discuss policies and perspectives while keeping in mind others' perspectives and situations.*

Individuals Do Not Represent a Collective: People must not be judged by the actions of a government, religion, political affiliation, or other ways that they identify themselves. As educators and community members, we both have met people who felt that they had to apologize for their association with their country of origin—despite the fact that they themselves have done nothing wrong. *We acknowledge that there are world events and perspectives that have caused harm to others; no civilian should take blame nor criticism for this in our spaces.*

The Power of Language: Educators must intentionally reflect on language used and be open to learning about their own biases through interactions with others. This is a situation in which we need to be open to listening and honoring others' voices—even if it may be uncomfortable. Some words or phrases that may have been the norm years ago are now considered slurs or disrespectful to different groups of people. Establishing a safe and honest environment in which students can teach one another (and educators!) about languaging surrounding their cultures without fear is critical. *Language is powerful and can either be something that unites or divides people.*

Listen and Learn: As educators, we must navigate the paths of learner and teacher simultaneously. We facilitate experiences that guide learning for our students and we share what we know about our content and from life experiences. We learn from our students about different perspectives, how to revisit our own biases, and how to best meet unique needs of the students we currently teach. Being a teacher who is humble enough to be a learner as well is critical to modeling the value of being a lifelong learner and that we appreciate the knowledge our students bring with them to our class.

Also important to note when embracing culturally responsive pedagogy is that students' goals and futures are diverse based on a variety of factors. Furlong and Orange-Jones (2025) argue that educators must reflect on their own views of "success" through a lens of understanding that they are not the only ways that one may be successful. Students' families may have different values surrounding their perspectives of what it means for their children to be successful; we consider this when counseling or advising students on their future.

It's important to remember that all of these are successful:

They may be the first in their family to graduate high school.
They may go to community college.
They may learn a trade, earn a vocational certificate, or become an apprentice.
They may pursue higher education at a four-year university or college.
They may not graduate high school but earned their GED (graduate equivalent degree).
They may speak more than one language.
They may have achieved a level of literacy that supports them in a career or job.
They may work at an entry-level position with potential.

They may contribute to the survival of their family.
They may be charitable and kind humans.
They may follow family traditions, religious customs, and are respectful of their elders.
They may aspire to become United States citizens (or not).
They may pass their courses and grades may be something they strive for.

The most important aspect of culturally responsive pedagogy is the positioning and languaging of the teacher. The teacher is a learner, a facilitator, and a listener. The teacher builds on what the students bring to the table. The teacher values all students and their unique talents and gifts. The teacher provides space to celebrate and amplify all voices. The teacher ensures that language oppression is not a variable in the classroom (Spina, 2025). When the teacher models these attributes, all stakeholders follow suit and they foster a culture of respect and belonging.

Conclusion

The journey through this chapter has demonstrated that the term **citizen** is far more complex than a simple legal definition. While documentation and the rights it confers are significant, a richer understanding of citizenship must also encompass character, civic engagement, and a commitment to justice. From the colonists who fought for their rights without representation to the enslaved people who used the legal system to claim their freedom, our history is a testament to the power of civic action that transcends legal status.

This complex reality places a unique and profound responsibility on educators. Teaching civics is not merely about reciting laws or celebrating historical victories; it is about creating a safe, inclusive space where students can explore tough questions and engage in respectful discourse. By embracing a culturally responsive pedagogy and modeling intellectual humility, teachers can guide students to see themselves not just as future voters, but as active participants and shapers of our society. In doing so, we move beyond the black-and-white view of citizenship and empower all learners to contribute to the ongoing story of our democracy, proving that a true citizen is defined by what they do, not just by what they are called.

References

Bauml, M., Quinn, B. P., Blevins, B., Magill, K. R., & LeCompte, K. (2021). "I really want to do something": How civic education activities promote thinking toward civic purpose among early adolescents. *Journal of Adolescent Research*, 38(1), 110–142. https://doi.org/10.1177/07435584211006785 (Original work published 2023)

Beadie, N., Burkholder, Z., Anderson, J. D., Hartman, A., Parker, W. C., & Steineker, R. (2021). From the diffusion of knowledge to the cultivation of agency: A short history of civic education policy and practice in the United States. *Educating for Civic Reasoning and Discourse*, 109–155. https://naeducation.org/wp-content/uploads/2021/04/NAEd-Educating-for-Civic-Reasoning-and-Discourse.pdf#page=122

Blevins, B. (2022). Action civics as a powerful tool. *Democracy and Education*, 30(2), 1–6. https://democracyeducationjournal.org/home/vol30/iss2/5

DeJaeghere, J. (2013). Critical civics and citizenship education: What kind of 'active citizen'? *Curriculum Perspectives*, 33(1), 83–86.

DiSalvo, Carl. (2022). Design as Democratic Inquiry: Putting Experimental Civics into Practice. MIT Press.

Furlong, D. (2022). *Voices of newcomers: Experiences of multilingual learners*. EduMatch.

Furlong, D., & Orange-Jones, K. (2025). *Learners first: Purpose and practicality in your early years of teaching*. Corwin.

Malin, H. (2011). American youth's civic purpose and participation: Patterns of community involvement and political action. *Applied Developmental Science*, 15(3), 111–124. https://doi.org/10.1080/10888691.2011.587720

Merriam-Webster, Incorporated. (n.d.). *Merriam-Webster.com dictionary*. Retrieved November 23, 2025, from https://www.merriam-webster.com/

Spina, C. (2025). *Igniting real change for multilingual learners*. Routledge.

U.S. Citizenship and Immigration Services. (n.d.-a). *10 Steps to naturalization*. U.S. Department of Homeland Security. Retrieved November 22, 2025, from https://www.uscis.gov/citizenship/learn-about-citizenship/10-steps-to-naturalization

U.S. Citizenship and Immigration Services. (n.d.-b). *Green Card eligibility categories*. U.S. Department of Homeland Security. Retrieved November 22, 2025, from https://www.uscis.gov/green-card/green-card-eligibility-categories

Westheimer, J., & Ladson-Billings, G. (2024). *What kind of citizen?: Educating our children for the common good*. Teachers College Press. https://books.google.com/books?hl=en&lr=&id=W_UOEQAAQBAJ&oi=fnd&pg=PP1&dq=connotations+of+the+word+citizen+in+the+united+states+civics&ots=ZflluImevV&sig=Wg8TmvUKOynFZaJr8mIRBqUYHNg#v=onepage&q=connotations%20of%20the%20word%20citizen%20in%20the%20united%20states%20civics&f=false

3

The Matrix

Introduction

We play the long game in education. As an institution, we are presented with babies who haven't lost their milk teeth yet, who can't tie their shoes or blow their noses. Then, over the course of 13 years, we transform them into contributing members of society, capable of working, learning more, and voting. We do this in a million ways, both large and small.

It is tempting to view civic education solely through the lens of content: historical facts, governmental structures, and founding documents. Yet, if we are to take Frederick Douglass's wisdom seriously, "It is easier to build strong children than to repair broken men," we must recognize that effective citizenship is not merely about *knowing* the facts, but about mastering the skills to apply them.

When we sat down to determine what were the key competencies that a person needed to master in order to become informed, active, and enthusiastic citizens of this nation, we came up with six. The first element is civic knowledge. Citizens need to know how the government works, what its components are, and what their rights and responsibilities are as citizens. The second is community engagement. Citizens need to be plugged

DOI: 10.4324/9781003746614-3

into their communities, to know the strengths and challenges, and to be willing to take action to affect those challenges. The third element is ethical decision-making. Do our students know about values, ethics, and how leaders and professional organizations make their decisions based on those values and ethics? The fourth element is critical thinking. Citizens should be able to navigate the information they are given, be skeptical about propaganda, and courageously think for themselves with the ability to provide evidence for their actions. Next is the element of national and global awareness. Students are already global citizens, but it's important for them to recognize the forces and bodies that guide their daily lives in the national and international spheres and how those bodies work with each other. Finally, is the ability to celebrate differences, to recognize that people come from different lived experiences, have different perspectives, and that we don't need to agree all the time, but respect and celebrate that differences are what make this country great.

So the challenge was how do we, as educators, make sure that students develop the skills that allow them to enter the world ready to hit the ground running, understand the way the world works, and take responsibility for their actions? The answer was the **Portrait of a Citizen Matrix**, the foundational tool of this framework. It is the answer to a crucial question: What, precisely, must a young adult be able to *do* to transition from a passive resident to an engaged and effective participant in a self-governing society?

The Matrix moves beyond generic terms like "responsible" or "critical" by organizing the essential civic skills into a clear, measurable structure. It is your department's common language for defining, teaching, and assessing civic readiness. Over the next pages, you will explore the six Core Competencies and their associated thirty **"I Can"** Statements, transforming the abstract goal of good citizenship into a tangible, achievable curriculum. This Matrix is not a mandate; it is the blueprint for building strong citizens.

Defining the Matrix: With Help from Merriam-Webster

The concept of a "matrix" is central to this framework, embodying a dual purpose:

1. **Origin and Development:** The matrix is the **place or point from which something else originates, takes form, or develops**. In this context, it's the core structure from which a well-rounded and engaged citizen emerges. It provides the essential ingredients—the competencies and skills—necessary for civic life to take root and flourish.
2. **Structured Array:** The matrix is also a **rectangular array** that organizes information clearly. Here, it arranges **six core civic competencies** and **five associated skills** for each, providing a systematic and measurable representation of civic development.

This Portrait of a Citizen Matrix is intentionally built this way: it is both the **catalyst** for civic growth and the **clear map** that guides the journey.

The Six Core Competencies

The matrix is built upon **six core competencies** that define a fully engaged citizen. These competencies are the broad areas of civic life where learners must demonstrate proficiency:

- **Civic Knowledge:** Understanding the foundational structures, history, rights, and current events necessary for informed participation.
- **Community Engagement:** Participating actively in community life, problem-solving, and advocating for positive change.
- **Ethical Decision-Making:** Demonstrating integrity, empathy, and responsibility when navigating complex situations and competing values.

- **Critical Thinking:** Analyzing information, identifying biases, and forming well-reasoned, independent opinions.
- **National and Global Awareness:** Recognizing the interconnectedness of local, national, and global issues and applying systems thinking to problem-solving.
- **Differences Celebrated:** Collaborating with diverse groups, actively listening, and valuing unique perspectives and lived experiences.

The Matrix: Portrait of a Citizen Competencies and Skills

Civic Knowledge: The Learner Exhibits Understanding of Government, History, Rights, Responsibilities, and Current Events (Table 3.1).

TABLE 3.1 Skills of Civic Knowledge

CK1	**Governmental literacy** I can accurately identify and describe the foundational structures, functions, and key branches of government (local, state and federal), explaining their roles and relationships.
CK2	**Historical contextualization** I can analyze significant historic events, movements, and figures and their impact on contemporary society, government, and individual rights.
CK3	**Rights and responsibilities application** I can articulate individual rights and liberties and describe responsibilities of citizens within a democratic society.
CK4	**Current events analysis** I can identify, synthesize, and evaluate information from various sources regarding current local, national, and world events and their impact on civic life.
CK5	**Civic engagement preparedness** I can identify and explain various pathways for civic participation and advocacy, explaining how individuals can contribute to their communities and larger society.

Community Engagement: The Learner Participates in Community Life, Problem-Solving, and Advocacy for Positive Change, and then Takes Action (Table 3.2).

TABLE 3.2 Skills of Community Engagement

CE1	**Community needs identification and analysis** I can assess my local community to identify unmet needs, potential challenges, existing assets and the impact of these issues on members of the community.
CE2	**Collaborative problem-solving and planning** I can collaborate with community stakeholders to brainstorm solutions to identified community problems, and create an action plan that takes diverse perspectives and available resources into consideration.
CE3	**Advocacy and persuasive communication** I can research and design a positive change with evidence-based examples and advocate for this change with the relevant audience to make it possible.
CE4	**Action implementation** I can actively participate and contribute to initiatives designed to address identified community needs.
CE5	**Showcase, reflection and impact assessment** I can showcase my results to classmates and community members, and reflect upon the process of community action, the impact of my efforts, and my growth as a citizen.

Ethical Decision-Making: The Learner Demonstrates Integrity, Empathy, and Responsibility in Interactions, Balancing Competing Values, Coming to Consensus, Changing Your Mind, and Compromising (Table 3.3).

TABLE 3.3 Skills of Ethical Decision Making

EDM1	**Value recognition and prioritization** I can identify competing values inherent in complex situations and thoughtfully consider how different people or groups might prioritize certain values over others.
EDM2	**Ethical principles application** I can identify and apply core ethical principles to analyze real-world problems.
EDM3	**Perspective taking and empathetic reasoning** I can understand the positions of others involved in an ethical dilemma or conflict and consider potential impacts on different individuals and communities.

TABLE 3.3 (Continued)

EDM4	**Collaborate resolution and adaptability** I can engage constructively in discussions to resolve a conflict, look for compromise and commonality, create consensus, and be open to changing my mind when new information emerges.
EDM5	**Responsible action and accountability** I can take responsibility for my decisions and actions and strive to understand the short-term and long-term consequences on others.

Critical Thinking: The Learner Analyzes Information, Identifies Bias, Forms reasoned opinions, Identifies Conflicts of Interest, and Identifies Uses of Propaganda (Table 3.4).

TABLE 3.4 Skills of Critical Thinking

CT1	**Information analysis and evaluation** I can effectively break down complex information from various sources (textual, visual, digital, AI), identifying key arguments, evidence, and possible influencing factors.
CT2	**Bias and perspective recognition** I can identify different types of bias within information, distinguish between fact and opinion, and recognize perspective and context.
CT3	**Reasoned opinion formation** I can synthesize and analyze information and evidence and create a well-supported opinion while acknowledging counter arguments.
CT4	**Conflict of interest identification** I can recognize and explain various conflicts of interest and how these conflicts can influence decisions and actions.
CT5	**Propaganda and manipulation detection** I can identify common propaganda techniques in the media and explain how these techniques are designed to persuade or manipulate audiences.

National and Global Awareness: The learner can recognize the interconnectedness of global issues and effectively problem-solve using systems thinking and an understanding of cause-and-effect relationships, treaties, and international bodies (Table 3.5).

TABLE 3.5 Skills of National and Global Awareness

NGA1	**Interconnectedness recognition** I can explain how local, national, and global issues are interconnected, and how events or policies in one area can have a ripple effect on other areas.
NGA2	**Global systems analysis** I can identify and describe the roles and functions of major international organizations and key international agreements, explaining their significance in addressing global challenges.
NGA3	**Cause-and-effect in complex systems** I can analyze complex national and global problems by identifying multiple causes, predict short- and long-term effects, and recognize feedback loops within these systems.
NGA4	**Multi-level governance understanding** I can differentiate between the different jurisdictions and responsibilities of local, state, and national governments, and explain how these governments interact with each other and with international bodies to address national and global issues.
NGA5	**Global problem-solving approaches** I can propose and evaluate different approaches to addressing national and global challenges, considering diverse perspectives, ethical implications, and effectiveness of certain strategies.

Differences Celebrated: The learner works with people of different ages and backgrounds. They celebrate unique perspectives and lived experiences by actively listening, expanding their beliefs, and making connections with others (Table 3.6).

TABLE 3.6 Skills of Differences Celebrated

DC1	**Inclusive collaboration** I can work in diverse groups, showing respect for others and integrating contributions from individuals of different ages, cultural backgrounds, and lived experiences.
DC2	**Active listening and empathy** I can actively listen to and strive to understand perspectives and lived experiences that differ from my own and avoid making assumptions based on previously held beliefs.
DC3	**Expanding beliefs and open-mindedness** I can articulate how interacting with diverse groups has allowed me to challenge or expand my beliefs, understandings, or prior assumptions.

TABLE 3.6 (Continued)

DC4	**Bridging divides and making connections** I can initiate and foster positive relationships with individuals from various backgrounds and contribute to a sense of community across differences.
DC5	**Honoring diverse action** I can promote and celebrate diverse pathways for civic action and engagement, recognizing and valuing contributions for all community members.

Mirroring What Educators Already Know

For educators and administrators, adopting a new framework can feel daunting. That's why the Portrait of a Citizen Matrix is intentionally designed to mirror and integrate with systems you already trust. This is not a competing model; it is the Civic Dimension of the larger educational conversation already happening across the country.

The Matrix aligns directly with the national movement for "Portrait of a Learner" (PoL) or "Portrait of a Graduate" (PoG) models. This strategic alignment ensures that civic readiness is not an assumed outcome, but an intentional and measurable goal integrated into the school's core vision.

The shared purpose and structure is clear: like the PoL/PoG, the framework redefines student success beyond test scores. It is competency-based, articulating the holistic knowledge, skills, and dispositions students need for success in life, career, and, most importantly, as self-governing citizens (Table 3.7).

TABLE 3.7 Chart of Interconnection between Portrait of a Citizen and Common Portrait of a Learner/Graduate

Portrait of a Citizen Competency	*Common Portrait of a Learner/Portrait of a Graduate Competency*	*Interconnection and Alignment*
Civic knowledge	Knowledgeable & Empowered Learner	Ensures that foundational academic content (history, government) is learned with the intent of real-world application for civic life.

TABLE 3.7 (Continued)

Portrait of a Citizen Competency	*Common Portrait of a Learner/Portrait of a Graduate Competency*	*Interconnection and Alignment*
Community engagement	Collaboration/ Community Contribution	Measures the practical application of skills by taking informed action to improve local or global society.
Ethical decision-making	Ethical Leader/Global Steward	Captures the essential social-emotional competencies like integrity, empathy, and responsibility, which are crucial for collaboration and leadership.
Critical thinking	Critical Thinker/ Problem-Solver	Directly measures the analytical and evaluative skills necessary to process civic information and solve community problems.
National and global awareness	Global Citizen/ Interconnected Learner	Measures the understanding of complex global systems, which is a common requirement for 21st-century readiness in an interconnected economy.
Differences celebrated	Culturally Competent/ Effective Communicator	Reflects the need for diverse collaboration, active listening, and bridging divides—foundational skills for a modern workforce and diverse democracy.

The Power of "I Can" Statements

Within each of the six competencies are five specific, measurable skills. Crucially, these skills are expressed as **"I Can" statements**. This strategic phrasing places the **learner at the center** of the educational experience, fostering *ownership* and *self-efficacy*. It will be possible for teachers to share this matrix with their students to have them self-assess where they are on this journey and what they still need to know.

By stating the skill as, for example, "I can accurately identify and describe the foundational structures, functions, and key branches of government" (CK1), the focus shifts from simply being *taught* the material to actively *acquiring* and *demonstrating* the ability. This approach makes the matrix a direct tool for students to track their own growth and for educators to design targeted, student-centered learning experiences.

Alignment with the NCSS C3 Framework

The Portrait of a Citizen Matrix is designed to work in conjunction with national standards for social studies education. Specifically, it aligns with the **National Council for the Social Studies (NCSS) College, Career, and Civic Life (C3) Framework for Social Studies State Standards**.

The C3 Framework (2013)) emphasizes the **Inquiry Arc**, which is a process built on four dimensions:

1. Developing Questions and Planning Inquiries
2. Applying Disciplinary Concepts and Tools
3. Evaluating Sources and Using Evidence
4. Communicating Conclusions and Taking Informed Action

The Portrait of a Citizen Matrix is strategically aligned with the NCSS C3 Inquiry Arc, ensuring a robust, skills-based approach to civic learning. The Civic Knowledge competency supports Dimension 2 (Applying Disciplinary Concepts and Tools) by grounding students in government and history. Critical Thinking aligns with Dimension 3 (Evaluating Sources and Using Evidence), fostering the ability to form reasoned opinions. The Ethical Decision-Making competency is integral to the thoughtful application of concepts and the responsible taking of informed action, bridging multiple dimensions. National and Global Awareness expands the scope of inquiry and application to complex, interconnected systems, relevant to both Dimension 1 (Developing Questions) and Dimension 2. Finally, Community Engagement directly connects to the ultimate goal, Dimension 4 (Communicating Conclusions and Taking Informed Action), while Differences Celebrated is essential for collaborative inquiry, evaluating diverse perspectives (Dimension 3), and engaging constructively during informed action (Dimension 4).

By adopting this matrix, educators, departments, and districts can be confident that they are providing a robust, skill-based curriculum that prepares students for college, career, and, most importantly, **a lifetime of meaningful civic engagement**

Alignment with the Roadmap for Educating for American Democracy

The Roadmap for Educating for American Democracy (EAD) is a landmark, cross-ideological inquiry framework designed to strengthen history and civic learning for all K-12 students. Created by a diverse group of over 300 scholars, educators, and practitioners, it is a national call to action to re-prioritize and invest in civics education to support a healthier constitutional democracy.

The EAD Roadmap is not a national curriculum or a set of standards. Rather, it is an advisory document that provides guidance for states, districts, and educators to transform their own curricula. It achieves this by shifting instruction from a focus on breadth to depth and integrating history and civics through inquiry.

The Portrait of a Citizen Matrix aligns with the EAD Roadmap. The EAD Roadmap is a broad framework that provides the content (seven themes and driving questions) for integrating history and civics. Both share a vision for developing informed citizens through inquiry and competency-driven learning. The EAD Roadmap (2021) calls for local education agencies to "Develop a Civic Learning Plan that lays out its goals, key performance indicators for measuring progress, and the operational plan for achieving civic excellence" which is exactly what the Portrait of a Citizen Matrix does. It provides the skills (competencies and "I Can" statements) necessary for students to successfully learn civic content and take informed action.

Onward!

Above all, this framework goes hand-in-hand with the best guidance we have at the district, state, and national level. The difference is that the Matrix gives you the practical, measurable steps necessary to teach the skills. The next chapters will introduce you to each of the competencies and skills in detail. You will find that some of these skills you build every day in your classrooms, and some might be brand new. Each, however, is essential for active participation in today's society. It's a heavy responsibility, and, yet, what more noble way to make an impact on society than assuring it can sustain itself democratically? As the Chinese proverb says, "The best time to plant a tree was twenty years ago. The second best time is now."

References

Educating for American Democracy. (2021). *Educating for American Democracy: Excellence in history and civics for all learners* [Report]. https://www.educatingforamericandemocracy.org/the-report/

Matrix. (n.d.). *In Merriam-Webster.com dictionary*. Retrieved April 14, 2026, from https://www.merriam-webster.com/dictionary/matrix

National Council for the Social Studies. (2013). *College, career, and civic life (C3) framework for social studies state standards: Guidance for enhancing the rigor of K-12 civics, economics, geography, and history.*

4

Civic Knowledge

Foundations of a Functional Society

Introduction

Picture this: You teach in a rural vocational school in a county that doesn't have a stop light. You're about to give your final exam in civics, and you've just passed out the test. One of your students, a boy who has decided to dye his hair three different colors for the occasion, shoots his hand up. When you call on him, he's confused about the section on Landmark Cases of the Supreme Court.

You clarify: "You need to take each Landmark case, write the constitutional problem, and then write what the majority opinion was. It should take a few sentences for each. For a bonus, you can mention what the dissent says."

The student looks at you, incredulous. "But that's too easy. Everyone knows that."

This actually happened to Darcy. And it was a wake-up call. Too often, civics instruction stops at the basic parts of the Constitution, treating knowledge as something that's "easy" to memorize. But as this student's response shows, a true understanding of civics requires so much more and this student was ready for it.

DOI: 10.4324/9781003746614-4

The last chapter introduced you to the Portrait of a Citizen Matrix. This chapter will now dive deeper into the first of those competencies: **Civic Knowledge**. We will move beyond the simple facts such as the three branches of government, historic movements, and rights and responsibilities and explore how a well-rounded citizen truly engages with their government.

Most people, when they think of civics class, they instantly think *boring*. But it doesn't have to be! A lot of civics instruction stops at the three branches of government, but there's so much more to being a citizen than understanding the basic parts of the Constitution. For example, how do the local, state, and federal governments interact with each other? Where do our tax dollars go? What happens when parts of the government aren't working together, or the way they are supposed to? Maybe even more importantly, what happens when the laws are unjust or unfair?

We also need to talk about rights *and* responsibilities. We study the Bill of Rights as if it were gospel, but how much do we talk about the responsibilities of citizens, including the responsibility to vote, to serve in the military, to pay our taxes, to serve on a jury, or even something as simple as obeying the laws. Then there are things that as citizens we *should* do that would make our communities better places, like contacting our elected officials to express our views, attend community meetings like school board meetings or town hall events, or even joining community or volunteer groups.

Just a quick note before we dive in. If you have a strategy that already has your students engaged and enthusiastic about civic education, by all means, stick with it! This guide isn't meant to be an all-knowing, top-down instruction manual. Instead, think of it as a toolkit. If you're looking for new ideas, need to liven up some of the material, or are searching for ways to make your lessons more engaging, then these suggestions are here for you to use.

Time to Reflect: *What are your strengths teaching civic knowledge in your classroom? What are some challenges you face? What are some questions you may have?*

The First Competency: Civic Knowledge

Civic Knowledge: The learner demonstrates deep understanding of government, history, rights, responsibilities, and current events of citizens of the United States.

Associated Skills

To achieve this competency, students will develop the skills detailed in Table 4.1.

TABLE 4.1 Skills of Civic Knowledge

CK1	**Governmental literacy** I can accurately identify and describe the foundational structures, functions, and key branches of government (local, state and federal), explaining their roles and relationships.
CK2	**Historical contextualization** I can analyze significant historic events, movements, and figures and their impact on contemporary society, government, and individual rights.
CK3	**Rights and responsibilities application** I can articulate individual rights and liberties and describe responsibilities of citizens within a democratic society.
CK4	**Current events analysis** I can identify, synthesize, and evaluate information from various sources regarding current local, national, and world events and their impact on civic life.
CK5	**Civic engagement preparedness** I can identify and explain various pathways for civic participation and advocacy, explaining how individuals can contribute to their communities and larger society.

Key Vocabulary from Merriam-Webster

Republic: a government in which leaders are elected by the people to represent them in order to make laws.

Democracy: a system of government where the people have the authority to make decisions about their government and lives.

Checks and Balances: a system in which one branch of government has the authority to block certain branches from an overreach of power, thereby making the branches of government co-equal.

Federalism: a system of government in which power is divided between the federal government and state governments.

Constitution: the supreme law of the land in the United States, also a collection of governing principles and laws that guide the government.

"Consent of the Governed": the theory that a government only has the power to rule if it has the approval of the people that it is governing.

Skill CK1. Governmental Literacy: I can accurately identify and describe the foundational structures, functions, and key branches of government (local, state and federal), explaining their roles and relationships.

Most people think that civics is just a dry list of facts, but it's actually a governmental system that affects all of us.

Let's start with foundational documents. When we talk about *Foundational Documents* we are talking about the documents that are the backbone of American law, and the way that these documents are interpreted is considered to be politics. Some have symbolic importance (like the Declaration of Independence) and some make the government actually work (like the Constitution.) Both documents show us who we are as a people, and set a very high bar as to where we want to be as a nation.

The Declaration of Independence: Our First Founding Document

The first document we need to talk about, of course, is the *Declaration of Independence*, which states:

> We hold these truths to be self-evident, that all men are created equal, that they are endowed by their Creator

> with certain unalienable Rights, that among these are Life, Liberty and the pursuit of Happiness.—That to secure these rights, Governments are instituted among Men, deriving their just powers from the consent of the governed,—That whenever any Form of Government becomes destructive of these ends, it is the Right of the People to alter or to abolish it, and to institute new Government, laying its foundation on such principles and organizing its powers in such form, as to them shall seem most likely to effect their Safety and Happiness.

Most people know the first line of this excerpt, but it's this whole excerpt that should be studied together, because what it gives us is the crux of what the Founders are aiming at; a new nation that is justifying its power from the "consent of the governed," that is, the people. Consider teaching about the philosopher John Locke who, in his *Second Treatise on Government*, introduces the term consent of the governed. One way that you can do that is to compare a short excerpt from Locke side-by-side with the Declaration's Preamble. Here's a short, accessible excerpt from Chapter 9 in *Second Treatise* (1689/2009):

> The great and chief end, therefore, of men uniting into commonwealths, and putting themselves under government, is the preservation of their property. To which in the state of nature there are many things wanting… Men, being all free, equal, and independent, no one can be subjected to the political power of another without his own consent. The only way anyone can give up his natural liberty and put on the bonds of civil society is by agreeing with other men to join and unite into a community for their comfortable, safe, and peaceable living… And thus that which begins and actually constitutes any political society, is nothing but the consent of any number of freemen capable of a majority to unite and incorporate into such a society. And this is that, and that only, which did, or could give beginning to any lawful government in the world.

TABLE 4.2 Grievances of the Declaration of Independence

Abuses of Power by King and Parliament	*Violations of Fundamental Rights*	*Actions Undermining Colonial Self-Governance*

The idea that the people have the say over who their leader is becomes the bedrock principle of the United States. This is what makes the Declaration of Independence the most quoted document in American history, and it is often quoted by other countries as well, especially when they are promoting democratic ideals and denouncing oppressive regimes.

The Declaration of Independence isn't just the preamble though; it's also the list of grievances that the united colonies make against the British King (George III) and Parliament. There are 27 grievances in the document, which are the reasons the colonies are leaving. The Preamble is the justification.

To help students truly grapple with the document's full meaning, consider these activities: Besides having students re-write the Preamble in their own words, think about having students make artistic representations of the Preamble. Also consider assigning one grievance per student and have them establish what each is saying (Table 4.2). Then you could have students categorize the grievances into three groups in a chart.

If some of the grievances fall into more than one category, work out with the class how to address that. Do you write the grievance across the two categories? Do you make it more of a Venn Diagram? Do you vote as a class about which category it fits in more? Make your decisions based on your class makeup.

Another way to help students grapple with the meaning of this document is to have them discuss the meaning of independence and if there are limitations to independence in government today. This could also serve as a great question for reflection for students.

Did you know? If you live in one of the original 13 states, there's a chance that the town that you work in has a hand-written copy of the Declaration of Independence in their archives. Once the Declaration was signed, it was sent to the printer in Philadelphia and then sent by riders to all the towns of the 13 colonies for a town leader to hand-copy the Declaration into the town records. This happened mid to late July, 1776. If your town was incorporated at the time of the Revolution, contact your town archives, historical society, or town manager to see if there's a copy available (Figure 4.1).

FIGURE 4.1 Students examining local handwritten copies of the Declaration of Independence at Nipmuc Regional High School. Students examining two Declarations of Independence from both towns of their regional school District. Both documents are dated July 17, 1776.

BEST Practices to Meet Diverse Needs of Learners

This is a section you will see throughout the book. All of these activities may be adjusted to give access and/or challenges to groups of students with diverse needs and you will find that many activity suggestions listed include different ways to engage in the assignment or task. It is important to give choice, when applicable, to provide students the opportunity to work to their strengths. Following are some recommendations for how to give access to the content for them—noting that many of these points of access may be relevant to any or all groups of students. Civics education MUST be accessible to all students.

- **Bridge** (English/multilingual learners): These students may benefit from videos that show role playing of examples in which participants are dramatizing the interactions of the different founders (potentially done by peers). This would provide the context, alongside facial and language cues, that may build the schema necessary to understand the different perspectives. Captions on the video would be helpful in connecting the vocabulary in writing to what is being said. Also, explicit use of maps and visuals throughout can establish geographical context as well.
- **Expand** (gifted students): Arranging for voting experiences within the school community and analyzing results with consequences for the results may be ways to engage students beyond the text. Also, role playing the interactions (see above) may provide these students with opportunities to engage more fully in the varying perspectives of stakeholders of the times.
- **Support** (students with learning challenges or differences): Graphic organizers and specific vocabulary (with visuals as needed) can clarify perspectives and unfamiliar words. Passages that depict the events written as first-person accounts (with frontloaded vocabulary highlighted and with word banks) can firmly establish the

experiences of all participants and students can complete graphic organizers with this information. Audios of the passages can be created by other students if appropriate.

- **Teamwork:** Role playing and recording as an age-relevant resource would be a way that these students can deepen their own understanding of the different perspectives of the participants in these events. This may be collaborative with different students writing and others taking roles in the production. Other students may choose to illustrate a book or story depicting one perspective or another.

> ***Spotlight on Newcomers:*** It's a tendency that we all have to assume that the students in front of us know the various histories or purposes of each of "our" holidays. But if a student has just arrived from another country they might not know what the Fourth of July celebrates (or other holidays specific to the United States), and at a certain point in the textbooks, it will no longer be taught. Don't miss this opportunity to share with newcomers about this holiday—and other patriotic or national holidays—and how they are celebrated. It's also important to ask newcomers to share with the class about a similar holiday (or similar document if they have one) from their country of origin.

The Constitution

The *Constitution* is the highest law of the land; all other laws need to comply with the laws in the *Constitution*, otherwise those laws are deemed unconstitutional and need to be thrown out. You will spend a lot of time on the *Constitution* and that's a good and necessary thing. The good news is that there are lots of sources on the *Constitution* and how to teach it.

Similar to when you're teaching the *Declaration of Independence*, it's important to back up a bit before diving into the *Constitution* head-first. Just like referencing John Locke before introducing the

Declaration of Independence, the philosopher that you really want to focus on when talking about the *Constitution* is Montesquieu. Baron de Montesquieu was a philosopher from France in the 18th century who thought deeply about how government should work. It was he who developed the theory of "separation of powers"—specifically, the three branches of government. It's a great conversation you can have with your class about the nature of power and why distributing it out is a better idea than concentrating it into one person or institution.

> In teaching history in NY, the Constitution is a foundational unit in both 7th and 11th grade. As part of this experience, I reached out to my local house reps who donated enough copies for each student to have a pocket Constitution. We would then have a Constitution ceremony in class where students promised to treat the Constitution with respect and reverence (never letting it touch the ground, not letting it fall apart, not losing it, etc.). They then signed their names in the back of their pocket Constitutions in permanent marker. Over the course of the unit, we continually referred back to the Constitution, underlining and annotating it. Every test for the rest of the year was "open Constitution" which allowed them to quote specific lines that helped support their historical claims. Segments of the Constitution became common refrains in the classroom and the students (in 7th and 11th grades!) were able to comfortably embrace this as a common text to quote. Most of the juniors continued to use their Constitution in their senior year government courses. One student in particular reported keeping her copy in her car because she said it made her feel safer in case she got pulled over.
>
> —Paige, teacher librarian

After you've talked about the underlying philosophical justification, you're also going to have to talk about the failed first Constitution, or the *Articles of Confederation*. Why do we discuss the Articles, especially knowing that they were a failure?

Learning from Our Mistakes: The Articles of Confederation

The Articles of Confederation were the first set of laws for a new United States of America from March 1781 to March 1789. The Articles were the law that the new states agreed upon and got them through the American Revolution. They were rooted in a vast dissemination of power, giving more power to each state rather than to a Federal Government. In this new federal structure, there was only one branch of government, a unicameral legislature. The Articles of Confederation were a knee-jerk reaction to the monarchy of England; what the founders discovered, however, was that when you disseminate too much power, if you spread it out too much, it becomes too difficult to make any decision. The result was a deadlock. The founders decided that they needed to meet again to revise the articles. The result was the Constitution.

It's not necessary to spend a long time on the *Articles of Confederation*, but it is important to teach about it for two reasons. The first reason is to show that the Constitution didn't magically spring out of thin air, that it was a series of trials and errors, and that the founders learned from the errors, which leads to the second reason, showing that governments make mistakes and that it's ok to fix them. Governments aren't perfect, just like people aren't perfect, and it's ok to make mistakes, learn from them, and move forward. To paraphrase the great Maya Angelou: When you know better, you do better.

On to the Constitution! As you know, the Constitution is divided into three distinct sections: The Preamble, the Articles, and the Amendments. It's a great idea to start with a Constitution inventory, having the students walk through the document to see what is there and why. There are a lot of ways you can do this:

- ***Document Walk***: All American history textbooks have a copy of the Constitution somewhere in the text. You can start with your students by walking through and seeing what they notice. Consider handing out sticky notes to students to have them mark certain things that they see. They might notice the structure of the document as being unusual; they might notice the Roman numerals. You can keep a bank of things that they notice on the board or in a document that is projected on a screen, and then go over the things that they notice.
- ***Inventory***: Depending on their level of comfort, you can have students do a quick inventory on what each part of the Constitution addresses. For this activity, it often helps to have students work in pairs so that they can tackle the document together, and consider *purposeful partnering* for students who might struggle. You can hand out a worksheet with just the titles of each section, so students will know where to look and what to do. This will take a while, so plan accordingly.
- ***Visual Representation of the Constitution***: For those students who do better with a graph or a chart, consider combining the inventory above with a graphic representation below. You can grab a copy of the constitution from the National Constitution Center, and have students pop each article into a word count, divide by 4400 (the number of words in the Constitution before the Amendments), create a chart, and turn that chart into a circle graph (Table 4.3).

The circle graph will likely look something like Figure 4.2.

Best Practices to Meet Diverse Needs of Learners

- **Bridge** (English/multilingual learners): These students may need opportunities to build schema about the perspectives of different stakeholders in the nation at this time. This may come in the form of short videos

TABLE 4.3 Parts of the Constitution

Section of the Constitution	*Number of Words (x)*	*Percentage of words (x/4400 [a] 100)*	*Main Subject, Structure, or Power Addressed in Article*
Preamble	52	1.2	Introduction to the Constitution.
Article I	2,268	51.5	The Legislative Branch (Congress); powers and limits.
Article II	1,023	23.3	The Executive Branch (President); powers and duties.
Article III	375	8.5	The Judicial Branch (Supreme Court and lower courts).
Article IV	340	7.7	Relations among states and the federal government.
Article V	143	3.3	The Amendment Process (how to change the Constitution).
Article VI	177	4.0	Supremacy Clause, debts, and religious tests.
Article VII	24	0.5	Ratification (the number of states needed for approval).

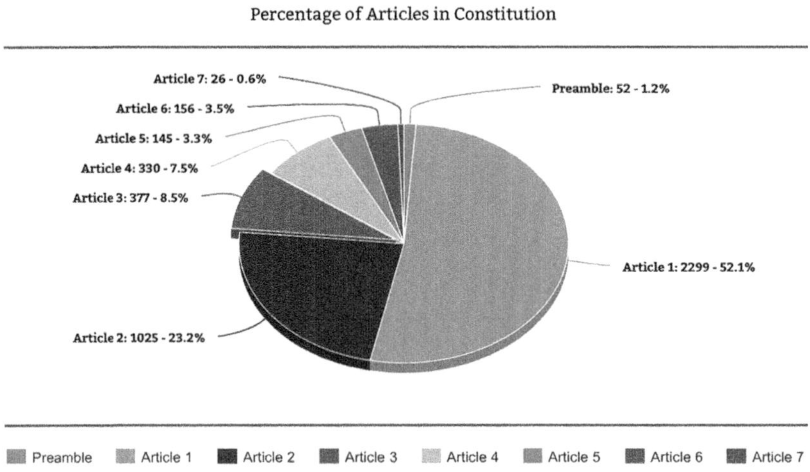

FIGURE 4.2 A circle graph representing the parts of the Constitution.

Note: This is only the parts of the original Constitution, before the amendments. In order to help your students grapple with what they are looking at, it helps to ask questions for them to answer such as: *Explain your Constitution Data in a paragraph format. Based on the data you've discovered, what does the Constitution do? Which section has the most amount of words? What topic does this section contain? What does this say about the priorities of the Framers—what was most important to them?*

with subtitles, graphic novels, or comics that illustrate the events of this time, or annotated notes with key vocabulary.

- **Expand** (gifted students): Students can look at the different parts of the constitution through the lens of a historian from today to see what was potentially the most impactful throughout different points in history. They can consider adding on to the Constitution—What may be things that our Founding Fathers should have included at this time and why? What may be the long-term effects of what may have been omitted? How would things be different if they were included?
- **Support** (students with learning challenges or differences): A jigsaw approach in which groups of students each work on a particular section of the Constitution and then come together to share what they found most important to understand. An opportunity to listen to a reading of parts of the Constitution may give students other modalities to understand it more fully.
- **Teamwork**: As a group, analyze the different amendments through the lens of the time period. Why are some before others, and what effects on historical events may these amendments have had? Create a visual or audial resource demonstrating the cause and effects.

The Constitution: A Closer Look at the Preamble and the Three Branches of Government

Now that your students have had a chance to explore the Constitution as a whole, it's time to dig into some of its most important features. We'll begin with the Preamble, the powerful introduction that sets the stage for the entire document.

Much like the Preamble to the Declaration of Independence, this opening statement provides the rationale and purpose behind the Constitution. It famously begins:

> We the People of the United States, in Order to form a more perfect Union, establish Justice, insure domestic

> Tranquility, provide for the common defence, promote the general Welfare, and secure the Blessings of Liberty to ourselves and our Posterity, do ordain and establish this Constitution for the United States of America.

You can use the same engaging strategies we discussed for the Declaration of Independence to explore this text. A fantastic way to ensure students understand the Preamble is to have them identify unfamiliar words and brainstorm their meanings together. Then, challenge them to rewrite the Preamble in their own words, which is a great way to assess comprehension. You could also ask them if anything is missing and should be added to the Preamble, if they were writing it today.

Making the Three Branches of Government Stick

The three branches of government are a cornerstone of civics education, and yet studies show that a bit less than one half of American adults can name all three (Annenberg, 2022). This statistic suggests that our teaching methods may not be as effective as they could be. To make this "boring but important" topic truly memorable and engaging, we need to go beyond the traditional lecture.

Here are some dynamic, hands-on ways to teach the three branches of government and the system of checks and balances:

- **Triads**: Divide students into groups of three. Assign each student a role: one for the Executive Branch, one for the Legislative Branch, and one for the Judicial Branch. Give them time to research the specific duties of their assigned branch using the Constitution and online resources. After their individual research, they can share their findings with their triad, teaching their peers about the other two branches. (Note for access: Different language and academic scaffolds or enrichment questions can be available for students as needed for each of these roles so students can self-monitor their learning.)
- **Whose Job Is It? (Flashcards)**: Create a game using either physical or digital flashcards. On each card, write a specific

government duty (e.g., "Vetoing a bill," "Declaring a law unconstitutional," "Writing new laws"). Challenge students to quickly yell out which branch is responsible for that action. This is a fast-paced and fun way to reinforce key responsibilities. (Note for access: This game may be played as a whole group or in smaller groups with built-in "wait time" for students who need processing time.)

- **Visual Representations or Analogies**: Ask students to create a visual representation of the three branches and explain how they work together. Encourage them to use a simple analogy, like a three-legged stool or a stoplight, to illustrate the concept. They should label the different parts of their visual with the names of the branches and their primary duties. (Note for access: Illustrations and labeling using single words or short phrases may be linguistic scaffolds that are appropriate for learners with diverse needs.)
- **Create a Song or Video**: Music is a powerful tool for memorization. Encourage students to create a song or a short video that explains the three branches of government and their respective duties. This creative project will help them internalize the information in a fun and lasting way. (Note for access: Songs often have shorter phrases and predictable repetition that can help multilingual learners and students with learning challenges engage more fully with the content.)
- **Stump the Teacher**: Nothing motivates students more than a chance to challenge their teacher. Have students create questions about the three branches of government to "stump" you. You could even invite a panel of other teachers to participate. Offer a prize for any student who asks a question you can't answer. This high-stakes game will encourage students to research deeply and ask hard questions. (Note for access: Students can play different roles in this game such as researchers, scribes, judges, or other ways to be involved.)
- **Video Games**: Supplement your lessons with educational video games. Websites like iCivics offer a great collection

of free games that allow students to interact directly with the concepts of government, including the three branches. These are perfect for reinforcing lessons or as a fun activity before a holiday (https://ed.icivics.org/games). (Note for access: The different modalities of language that these games provide are excellent for students to experience the concept in ways that are accessible.)

We want students to enjoy learning about the three branches of government and the essential system of checks and balances. The more they engage with and appreciate the Constitution, the more they will understand its importance and want to protect its principles. So, don't be afraid to get silly and have fun with it!

> **Time to Reflect**: *How much time do you spend on the underlying theoretical philosophy concerning self-rule, consent of the governed, and checks and balances? What may be the impact on other aspects of civics and history study if not enough time is spent on these concepts?*

The Electoral College: When the Popular Vote Is Just a Suggestion

So we all go to vote on election day, and it turns out that it's just a suggestion to the electors from our state how to vote. Great! (Please note the sarcasm.) This is a really hard concept for most students (and most Americans) to conceptualize. Only 40% of Americans can explain what happens if the Electoral College is tied (Pew Research Center, 2023).

It's an antiquated system, to be sure, but as of right now it's the only one we've got, so how do we teach it effectively?

- **School Elections, but Add an Electoral College**: This would be a great way to show the Electoral College in a "Winner Take All" fashion. It would require your class to be election central, to map out the classes, and to calculate both the popular vote and the electoral vote. Most schools (if they even have mock elections anymore, and if Mickey Mouse isn't declared the winner) only have a direct vote. Adding the Electoral College aspect will definitely help with the understanding of an electoral college.

- **Online Simulations**: Look for online simulations like 270towin.com and then have students make their own predictions, take a screen shot of it, and turn it in. Offer to them that if they get the map 100% that you will give out a prize.
- **Debate**: Now more than ever, it would be a good time to have students debate whether or not the Electoral College should be abolished. It does not have to be in a debate format, but could be in a format that allows for more discussions. Look in later chapters for more ideas!
- **Exceptions to the Rule**: Don't forget to talk about states that have split electors (like Maine and Nebraska) and take a few moments to talk about what happens with *faithless electors*, or if the Electoral College deadlocks in a tie. These are rare, but they do happen, and remember, this might be the only time your students learn about the Electoral College. Don't cut corners.

Compromise Is Not a Dirty Word

Compromise in government is often today considered a weakness, but when 13 new states, from different areas of the country with different monetary interests and different ways of life, were vying for power and forging a new nation at the same time, compromise was necessary and important. Having said that, all of the compromises today aren't things we as a nation are proud of. It's important to show our history, warts and all, to teach the evolution of thought and how a country looks forward, not back. Our founders didn't get everything right, nor did they expect to. They did the best they could with what they had at the time. That's all we can hope to do, too.

In this section we will be discussing the *Great Compromise* and the *Three-Fifths Compromise*. When discussing the compromises, it's OK to include the *Bill of Rights* in the discussion, even though it comes after the Ratification of the original document. The reason being, a call for a national bill of rights was a part of the ratification debates and adding the first ten amendments (even though they weren't changes to the Constitution as much as additions) was the compromise to get the ratification through. Today we think of these things as foregone conclusions, but the founders had a healthy fear of anarchy and carefully weighed how to avoid armed uprisings by angry citizens.

Remember that in a compromise, *no one gets everything they want*.

The Great Compromise: Important here is to focus on the two plans, the Virginia Plan and the New Jersey Plan, including the key players and the key elements. A good way to teach this is to have students fill out a rather large Venn Diagram with each plan on either side. Then have the Great Compromise in the intersecting section between the two circles. You might end up with something that looks like Figure 4.3.

Go Deeper: coloring this would be a great way to show the compromise! Yellow for the Virginia Plan and Blue for the New

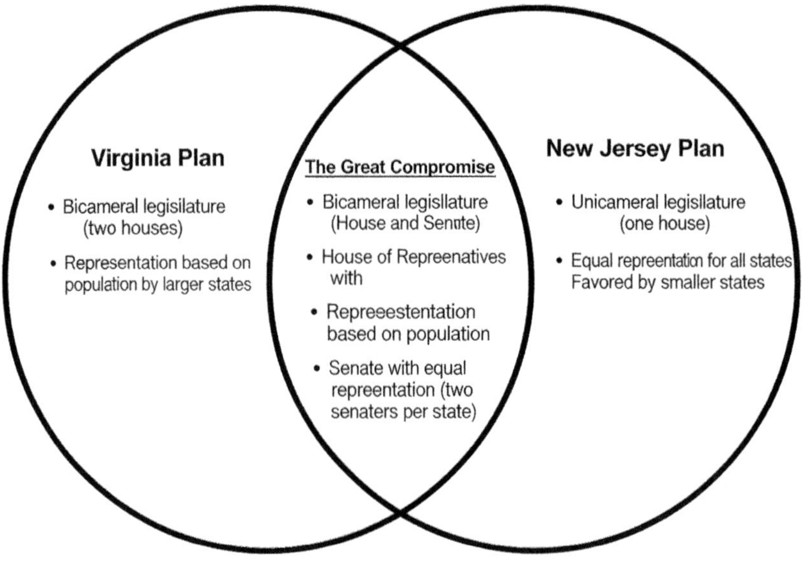

FIGURE 4.3 The great compromise Venn Diagram.

Please note, original spelling.

Jersey Plan, with Green as the Great Compromise would show the blend of the two plans.

The Three-Fifths Compromise: The Three-Fifths Compromise remains a profound stain on our nation's history. It was an appalling political calculation about how to count enslaved people for both tax purposes and representation in the House of Representatives. As you teach this topic, it is important to state plainly that this was a terrible idea; one that unfairly tipped political power to the southern states in Congress. A powerful activity is to have students examine data from the 1790 census to see how not counting enslaved people, counting all of them, and applying the three-fifths rule dramatically shifted the balance of power. A compelling way to further engage students is to have them imagine and reflect on a pivotal "What if?" scenario: What might have happened if enslaved people were not included in the count for representation at all? Would the nation still have been torn apart by the Civil War?

Ratification Debates and the Bill of Rights: The Constitution, once approved by the delegates, was anything but a foregone conclusion; it required ratification by 9 of the 13 states to become law. This period of intense debate is an excellent opportunity for students to look at the original document and identify what they feel is missing. This naturally leads into a discussion about the importance of including a Bill of Rights as an integral part of the Constitution. You can then challenge students to consider a hypothetical: What would be the implications if the Bill of Rights were a separate document, and which would be more powerful, the Constitution or a standalone Bill of Rights? The Ratification Debates also provide the perfect context to introduce the Federalist Papers, with excerpts from the most referenced papers, such as numbers 10, 51, and 78, serving as powerful primary sources. We will have more discussion of the Bill of Rights later in the chapter, when we discuss *Rights and Responsibilities of Citizens*.

How a Bill Becomes a Law: A lot of teachers play the famous cartoon from *Schoolhouse Rock* and call it a day. Starting with the cartoon isn't a bad idea, but students really need to learn more about how a bill becomes a law than a three minute cartoon!

Here are some interesting ways to get students to engage with the legislative process:

Flowcharts: Have students create a flowchart of steps from Introduction to the President's signature (including the possibility of VETO from the President and override from Congress). Or, hand students an envelope of the stages cut into squares and have them arrange the steps in order. Once you've checked it, they can paste it onto a piece of construction paper.

Comic Strips: Give students the opportunity to create their own comic strips, by first storyboarding the legislative process, and then creating a comic strip.

Role Playing: Assign roles of legislators and President, and have students enact how a bill goes through the legislative process to become a law.

Try this Powerful Extension: Proactive, Reactive, and Retroactive Laws

When we are teaching about how a bill becomes a law, it is important to talk about the role of laws in society. Lawmakers don't just make laws to look good (or to make their opponents look bad); they make laws to create change. When talking about proactive, reactive, or retroactive laws, giving a good example really helps. A good example of a proactive law might be seatbelt laws, where a good example of a reactive law might be child labor laws. A retroactive law is harder because they don't happen often, but decriminalizing something might be a good example. For example, in many states, helmets are no longer required for motorcycle operators. Once you teach this concept, this is an easy one that you can reinforce moving forward by asking the students about new laws and whether they are proactive, reactive, or retroactive.

Federalism: Federalism is the heart of American democracy; it allows for certain spheres of influence in the creation and execution of laws. In this vast country, one person, even one body, could not accurately or effectively make laws for every person. Imagine if there were just one law for traffic control, that encompassed the busiest city streets and the most rural one lane roads. Federalism breaks through the logjam, and, more importantly, it allows citizens to see the results of their choices when they go to vote. They get to see what happens at their schools as a result of the people they vote into the school board. They see the result of their taxes when it comes to road or bridge maintenance through their state representatives. And they get to see the results of international relations thanks to the person they vote into office as president. It could be said that the wholesale belief in federalism was the true genius of the founders. They knew that they wouldn't be able to understand all of the complications and intricacies of each corner of the United States, so trusting the local authorities to do their jobs, or "stay in their lane" helped to diffuse the power and make it work, all at once. This is a great time to talk about taxes!

Try this Extension: Laws don't just happen at the national level; they also happen at the local and state level. It is important for students to see how the legislative process is different between the national process, state process, and local process. Take time to discuss how laws are created in each sphere of their lives. A good way to discuss this is with scenarios asking students, "Who's in Charge?"

> I realized that I only taught about taxes one time all year, during the American Revolution, and in that context, taxes were treated as bad. I needed to show my students that taxes were necessary for governments to function properly and to make changes happen in our communities.
>
> —Anonymous teacher

Here are some other examples of ways to highlight the skill Governmental Literacy *in your classroom:*

- A student can describe the differences between local, state, and federal governments and explain where the jurisdictions overlap. This may be done in an essay format, a T-chart, a Venn Diagram, or any other visual.
- A student can explain the different roles in the local and state government and how to civically engage with local representatives. A "tree" or diagram of the actual names of people in these different roles may be a great resource to keep in the room.
- A student can observe a local council meeting or interview a representative about the responsibilities associated with their position and record a news report with their findings. Students can collaborate on potential questions to ask following the meeting.
- A student can explain the reasoning behind a dissenting opinion of a landmark case of the Supreme Court. Extensions may include opinions on hypothetical consequences if the decisions had been different.
- After reading the Declaration of Independence, students can have a Socratic Seminar on the meaning of independence—as a country, as a state, and as a human being.
- A student can research the roles and history of the two-party system and the current ways that these parties currently identify themselves.

Time to Reflect: *How much time do you spend talking about federalism, including the interaction between federal, state, and local governments? How can you include this into your regular lessons?*

Skill CK2 Historical Contextualization: I Can Analyze Significant Historic Events, Movements, and Figures

Contextualization means to study something within its historical place and time, not individually or without knowing the cause and effect. Consider when you have vocabulary terms at the beginning of each unit, asking students not just to give a one sentence answer, but to expand it out to three, for a Cause–Event–Effect scheme:

- *What caused this to happen? (Cause)*
- *What is the historical event? (Event)*
- *What did this historical event cause to happen? (Effect)*

Let's look at the example of the Boston Tea Party:

The Boston Tea Party

What caused it? (Cause): *Boston colonists were angry about a three cents tax on tea, after the Townshend Acts and the Boston Massacre happened in the city. They did not want to pay the extra tax because they connected the levying of taxes to oppression. They wanted a say in how they were taxed.*

What was it? (Event): *On December 16, 1773, dozens of Boston men, some dressed as Indigenous Americans, boarded three ships owned by the British East India Company and threw 342 chests of tea into Boston Harbor.*

What it caused? (Effect): *This destruction of property was so expensive and made legislators in Great Britain so angry, that Parliament decided to punish Boston with the series of acts known as the Coercive Acts, which included closing the Boston Harbor to trade, closing all public meeting spaces, sending over troops, replacing the governor with a general, and re-instituting the Quartering Act where soldiers could live with civilians in their own homes.*

If you did it the "old way," for vocabulary, the answer would only be the middle entry. Adding the cause and effect gives it more *context*. This can be done for almost all of your historical vocabulary. Yes, it takes more time, but it also helps students to anchor these events to others, and sets up the idea of cause-and-effect, in their minds. By putting historic events in their context, it highlights not only their importance but also the interconnectedness of events. For all students, this type of structure when learning builds schema and encourages this type of security for the future as they view events in other areas and events of their lives.

Amendments: Everyone Makes Mistakes in their Time and Place

All too often, civics education focuses on the first ten amendments and then moves on. This is a missed opportunity to show students that the Constitution is a living document—one that has evolved to fix its mistakes and adapt to new challenges. While some amendments may seem like "deep cuts" (we're looking at you, Eleventh and Twentieth Amendments), there is value in teaching each one. It's also an excellent chance to explore a fascinating topic on its own: Why is our Constitution so difficult to change in the first place?

Growing Pains in the New Republic

The Eleventh and Twelfth Amendments are perfect examples of the Founders addressing problems they didn't anticipate. They show that as a new nation grappled with its identity and power dynamics, new laws were sometimes necessary.

The **Eleventh Amendment**, for instance, settles a fundamental question of state sovereignty: Can an individual sue an entire state? The answer, as the amendment clarifies, is no.

The **Twelfth Amendment** is even more applicable to a modern audience, as it addresses a major flaw in the original electoral system. The system was designed for a time without political parties, where the top vote-getter became president and the second-place finisher became vice president. This led to a dysfunctional partnership between political rivals like John Adams and Thomas Jefferson, whose bitter relationship undermined the Adams presidency and ended their friendship. Thanks to the Twelfth Amendment, electors now cast separate ballots for president and vice president, ensuring that a single, ideologically aligned team takes office.

The Reconstruction Amendments

The Thirteenth, Fourteenth, and Fifteenth Amendments rightly receive attention in the classroom because they are the constitutional answer to the questions left unresolved by the Civil

War. They overturn the shameful Three-Fifths Compromise by clarifying that every person counts as a whole person. While the Thirteenth Amendment is relatively straightforward in abolishing slavery, the Fourteenth Amendment is particularly "meaty" and deserves deeper study, especially when connected to modern Supreme Court decisions that rely on its Equal Protection and Due Process clauses. For the Fifteenth Amendment, a critical discussion point is who it leaves out—a significant portion of the population, including half the country, which was a source of widespread anger and a sense of betrayal.

The Progressive Era Amendments

The Seventeenth, Eighteenth, and Nineteenth Amendments are "fun to teach" because they brought about real and tangible change. The Eighteenth Amendment (Prohibition) is a fantastic case study in government overreach and unintended consequences, neatly tied to the repeal by the Twenty-first Amendment. The Seventeenth Amendment, which allows for the direct election of senators by the people, feels intuitively right to modern students. And, of course, the Nineteenth Amendment, which granted women the right to vote, is a cornerstone of American democracy.

But what about the Sixteenth Amendment? It's often the ugly duckling of the bunch because talking about federal income tax and wealth inequality isn't typically seen as exciting. However, this is a lost teaching opportunity. Who would argue that teaching about taxes isn't important, especially when most people feel they're overtaxed? If we don't teach students the importance of taxes, they will get that information from sources that are paid to slant their view.

> **Time to Reflect:** *What if the one change you made after reading this book was to teach more about taxes? What would that look like in your classroom? Can you predict how that would affect your students' understanding of government?*

Other Twentieth-Century Amendments

The Twentieth Amendment ties up the loose ends of a bygone era, shortening the time between a presidential election and the inauguration. With the advent of new innovations in travel and communications, the long four-month "lame duck" period became an unnecessary risk. A great way to gauge student understanding is to challenge them to draft a new amendment that further shortens or modifies this period, based on an even faster exchange of information (the internet) and travel (commercial airlines), which could set up a fantastic classroom debate.

The Twenty-second and Twenty-fifth Amendments are incredibly relevant today, establishing presidential term limits and a clear line of succession. Especially at a time when our presidents are setting new age records, these amendments might make students ask, "What took them so long?"

Finally, the Twenty-fourth and Twenty-sixth Amendments help to make voting more accessible and equitable. Teaching the Twenty-fourth Amendment alongside the Civil Rights Movement is essential for understanding the fight against voter suppression. Similarly, connecting the Twenty-sixth Amendment directly to the Vietnam War—the "old enough to fight, old enough to vote" argument—is key to promoting student comprehension.

Landmark Cases of the Supreme Court

Like the Amendments, your students will learn more about the government and how it works, and also how the Supreme Court works, if you teach the landmark cases in historical context, to explain not only how they were shaped by their times, but also how they caused change in both the short and the long term. Again, think Cause, Event, Effect. It's important to mention here that the dissenting opinions really do matter, and students should be able to read them as part of their understanding of the document. It will give them a whole new perspective that the winners don't always write the history, and that sometimes ideas are too soon for their time. A great resource for Landmark Cases of the Supreme Court is Streetlaw. Not only do they break down the case nicely, but they also have levelled reading so you can have a number of different abilities access the text at the same time, at their own level (www.landmarkcases.org).

SEL connection: Considering the amendments and landmark cases from the various perspectives of different stakeholders of the time would be a powerful activity to illustrate points of view through the lens of what people perceived was beneficial to the nation and to themselves personally. How might life have been different today if not for certain landmark cases or amendments? Are there any laws today that you think may be changed for the better in the future?

Marching for Centuries about Civil Rights

As long as there has been a United States, there has been a debate over who has the right to participate in government. It has been a long, hard-fought process for minorities to gain the same access to the legislature as the people who happened to look like the Founding Fathers. Consider ways that you can help connect the dots with students about this important aspect, in historical context. Nor was it just the important public speakers, but thousands of lesser-known individuals who made their displeasure with the United States government known. Don't just teach Frederick Douglass; also consider teaching Ellen and William Craft, who also escaped slavery, also went north, and also spoke about their experiences. Civil Disobedience is also as old as the nation, even before the ink dried on the Declaration of Independence. Have students really drill down on the arguments of those who are pushing against the laws, and ask the students are the laws the problem, or are the people who are challenging them really asking too much?

Go Deeper: Share contemporary criticism of those who sought civil rights, to see what the criticism was in historical context. They might be surprised to see that some leaders who are lauded today, were arrested, beaten, and marginalized in their day.

Here are some more examples of ways to highlight the skill of ***Historical Contextualization*** *in your classroom:*

- A student can create a PowerPoint presentation on an enslaved worker rebellion and present it to the class.
- A student can rewrite the Gettysburg Address in their own words, through the lens of a different time period, or the perspective of someone who is analyzing the evolution of the role marginalized persons played through history
- A student can explain the dissenting opinion of a Supreme Court Case and why it is important.
- A student can create a visual comparison of the goals and results of an enslaved worker rebellion with the events of the Civil Rights Movement of the 1960s.
- A student can discuss how the Civil Rights Movement influenced current legislation regarding equality and civil liberties.
- A student can compare excerpts from "Civil Disobedience" by Henry David Thoreau and "Letter from a Birmingham Jail" by Martin Luther King.
- A student can write a poem from the historical perspective of someone from their time period of choice who does not feel that they experience "liberty, justice, or equality" in their lives.
- A student can create a list of suggested books of different genres that may support informal book studies/clubs on civil disobedience, civil rights, or a related topic.

Skill CK3. Rights and Responsibilities Application: I can articulate individual rights and liberties and describe responsibilities of citizens within a democratic society.

Beyond simply memorizing facts, it is more critical than ever that students understand their rights and responsibilities as citizens. This skill provides a powerful opportunity to discuss the foundational concepts of rights—including natural, universal, and individual liberties—and explore the rich debate surrounding their application. The phrasing "a democratic society" rather than "American society" is particularly powerful, as it highlights that these concepts are universal and generally accepted around the globe.

Let's start with the cornerstone of American liberties: the Bill of Rights. Thinking of it as a crucial checklist before a big event can help students grasp the importance of each amendment. These are the protected rights of all people in the United States, and because they are attached to the Constitution, they are fiercely protected by the Supreme Court. Here are some ideas for helping students grasp these concepts:

- **The Big Beautiful Bill of Rights Slideshow**: Have students create a slideshow for each amendment, including the original text, an explanation of its meaning, and associated images. For the final slide, students can write a paragraph on which amendment they believe is the most important, or argue why they are all equally vital.
- **A Day Without Rights**: In a reflective exercise, have students write a paragraph, essay, or create a vlog detailing what a day without the Bill of Rights would look like. What rights would they miss most, and what would they worry about in their daily lives?

Our department also did an annual project with the juniors of Supreme Court cases. Working in pairs, students chose a case, such as *Mapp* v. *Ohio*, from a list of options. They would then research the case and present their side to a panel of "justices" (other history teachers and building admin) who would then ask detailed follow-up questions: Did the school officials need probable cause or only reasonable suspicion? Could officials see cigarettes in the bag or did they have to remove the contents? If graffiti is written in blue pen ink and a student has a blue pen, does that make them guilty? Is there a difference between searching a purse vs. a book bag vs. a locker? After each side was presented and discussed, the class of

> students would then vote on what they believed should be the decision based on the Constitution. We would then reveal the actual vote and discuss why it might have been the same or different from the class decision. I loved this project as it really highlights the lived experience of the Constitution. We often talk about the lawmakers in Congress and the enforcement of the Executive branch. This was an engaging way to show how the laws and enforcement of them impacted everyday people and also highlighted how laws can be interpreted or deemed unconstitutional. It also lays the groundwork for highlighting what would happen when the system falls apart in history (such as when the courts sided against Jackson and he said let the courts enforce it) or in current events.
>
> —Paige, teacher librarian

With Liberty and Justice for All

It is easy to think of liberties and freedoms only as they apply to us personally. Have a frank conversation with your students about how these rights apply to everyone—even the weakest, the smallest, and the most vulnerable. Emphasize that it is the responsibility of all citizens to protect the rights of all people.

For a powerful extension, consider including the famous poem "First They Came" by Martin Niemöller. This piece serves as a poignant reminder that inaction in the face of injustice is a direct threat to the liberties of all.

FIRST THEY CAME By Martin Niemöller (1946)

First they came for the Communists and I did not speak out because I was not a Communist
Then they came for the Socialists and I did not speak out because I was not a Socialist
Then they came for the trade unionists and I did not speak out because I was not a trade unionist

Then they came for the Jews and I did not speak out because
I was not a Jew
Then they came for me and there was no one left to speak out
for me.

SEL connection: Discuss the ways that inaction may be more dangerous than action through references to this poem. What emotions may people have during times of inaction? Connect this to the notions of bystanders with respect to bullying.

The Bill of Rights illuminates both the ideas of Natural Rights and Individual Liberties, but the definition of each is slightly different. The idea is that Natural Rights is a set of accepted rights that everyone has just because they exist. Individual liberties are an agreed-upon set of rights that have been written down. They often overlap. Let's break down these concepts:

- **Natural Rights:** These are rights that every human being is entitled to at birth and are considered largely inalienable. The Declaration of Independence famously claims these to be "life, liberty and the pursuit of happiness."
- **Individual Liberties:** These are the specific rights enshrined in the Bill of Rights and other constitutional amendments, such as freedom of speech, freedom of religion, the right to peaceably assemble, and the right to bear arms.

To demonstrate the universality of these concepts, consider using documents beyond the Declaration of Independence and the Constitution. Comparing excerpts of these texts provides a rich discussion on the evolution of human rights over time and across different cultures. Key examples include:

Declaration of the Rights of Man and Citizen (1789) Written by the Marquis de Lafayette, it outlined the rights of French citizens and served as a preamble to the French constitution. It includes the rights to liberty, property, security, and resistance to oppression.

Declaration of the Rights of Women (1791) Also written in France, by Olympe de Gouge, it was a response to the Declaration of the Rights of Man.

Declaration of Sentiments (1848) Largely written by Elizabeth Cady Stanton at the Seneca Falls Convention, it mirrors the Declaration of Independence.

The Universal Declaration of Human Rights (1948) Post-World War II, this was adopted by the United Nations and acknowledges the rights of freedom of expression, freedom of movement, freedom from torture, freedom of religion, freedom to education, the right to seek asylum, and the right to marry.

BEST Practices to Meet Diverse Needs of Learners

- ♦ **Bridge** (English/multilingual learners (MLs)): Front-loaded vocabulary with visuals at the beginning of the unit may help build schema and help MLs make connections to their unique prior knowledge. (Do not assume that they have a background understanding of US politics or history). The America-specific notion of *liberty* may be challenging to understand in terms of other types of liberty. Sentence stems or frames, graphic organizers, and multilingual and visual word walls may all support independence in writing.
- ♦ **Expand** (gifted students): It is critical that extension activities are not simply extra or more lengthy assignments, but rather different types of challenges that engage students more deeply in the same concepts. This may look like conducting interviews with local civics experts regarding their views on liberty, debating different perspectives of historical events or issues, or writing poetry or songs that depict emotions that may have been felt behind the issues.
- ♦ **Support** (students with learning challenges or differences): These students may benefit from a visual and

audio representation of the Bill of Rights. Anchor charts with annotations or key words highlighted can help them identify important concepts to remember.

- **Teamwork**: Students may work in groups to add to the *First they came…* prose or write from the perspective of an outsider looking in on this point of view.

Beyond Rights: Embracing Our Responsibilities

With great rights come great responsibilities. Citizenship is not a free ride; citizens receive the benefits of a democratic society but must also contribute to its maintenance. This is an area that is often glossed over, but it presents a perfect opportunity for a meaningful lesson. We tend to assume that students will learn these responsibilities from other sources. But if they don't learn them from us, in a civic education class, where will they?

Teaching responsibilities is about empowering students to be active participants in their government. A discussion on this topic could cover:

- Voting in local and national elections.
- Serving on a jury when called.
- Staying informed on current events and public issues.
- Obeying laws and respecting the rights of others.
- Participating in community service.

A word about natural rights

Whether they are called Natural Rights, Unalienable Rights, or Human Rights, they are basically the same thing. The idea is that each person, just by being born, is entitled to respect and dignity that appreciates the integrity of their beings. Sam Adams said, "Among the natural rights of the colonists are these: First a right to life, secondly to liberty, and thirdly to property; together with the right to defend them in the best manner they can." Of course, Thomas Jefferson coined the term, "Life, Liberty and the Pursuit of Happiness," as unalienable rights. These are bedrock principles that have withstood the test of time, and when these ideas have been challenged, it has been to attempt to widen the circle of people who demand those rights. Nelson Mandela warned us that, "To deny people their human rights is to challenge their very humanity." And John F. Kennedy reminded us that "The rights of every man are diminished when the rights of one man are threatened."

Contrary to popular misconception, Natural Rights are a concept that students can grasp early, because it's the foundation of equality in schools. Don't be afraid to teach it.

Here are some examples of ways to highlight the skill ***Rights and Responsibilities*** *in your classroom:*

- Given a hypothetical scenario, a student can identify which constitutional rights might be relevant and explain the associated civic responsibilities.
- Students can create a game of Rights and Responsibilities of citizenship.
- Students can create a slideshow, news article, or visual representation of the Bill of Rights.
- Students can write a short essay on what Amendment (1–10) is the most important and why.
- Students can craft an argument for a more current list of the Bill of Rights.
- Students can annotate a visual of the Bill of Rights with their reflections, experiences, or opinions about each.
- Students compare two documents on human rights either in the form of a comparative essay, Venn Diagram, or T-chart, or by describing them using key words and phrases.
- Students can create a visual in which they illustrate the rights within the United States with the corresponding responsibilities that one has to support these rights.

- Students can debate the responsibilities they should have in participating in their school community and the rights that would come alongside those responsibilities. (Students can also discuss rights that they feel students should not have as well.)

Skill CK4. *Current Events Analysis: I can identify, synthesize, and evaluate information from various sources regarding current local, national, and world*

In an era of rapid information flow, the ability to critically analyze current events is no longer a luxury—it is a fundamental civic skill. Integrating current events into your curriculum is vital for showing students that the principles of government and history are not static concepts but are constantly at play in the world around them. This practice helps to cultivate engaged, informed, and responsible citizens who can connect classroom learning to their daily lives.

One effective strategy is to make a current events assignment a consistent weekly ritual. Better yet, make it as certain as death and taxes. The format can be simple and repeatable.

A Structured Approach to Current Events

On Sunday night or early Monday morning, choose a topic for the week. This could be a significant development that has just occurred or a major event on the horizon, such as the opening of the Olympics, a NATO summit, a natural disaster, or a new piece of legislation. Students are then asked to find and read an article on the topic, *providing a direct link to their source at the top of the page*. (This way you can read it too, to make sure that they were really able to access the material.) Following their reading, they respond to a set of guiding questions designed to build critical thinking skills:

1. **Synthesis: What is most important about what I've just read?** This question requires students to distill the main points and separate key information from minor details.
2. **Metacognition: What don't I understand?** This encourages students to be aware of their own knowledge gaps

and to formulate questions for further inquiry, rather than simply accepting the information as fact.

3. **Connection and Inquiry: What can I connect to, or what do I wonder about?** This prompts students to relate the event to historical context, personal experience, or other subjects, and to think beyond the immediate facts of the article.
4. **Bonus: What is my opinion on the subject?** By making this optional, you invite students to share their personal reflections once they've processed the factual information, fostering a safe space for respectful discourse.

Navigating Complexities and Media Literacy

To ensure students are successful, scaffolding is essential. On Monday morning, provide a brief historical overview of the event or conflict. A little context goes a long way in helping students understand the background and what to look for in their articles. On Friday, a current events "roundup" can serve as a capstone discussion. This provides an opportunity for students to ask questions, share insights, and engage with their peers.

It is crucial to explicitly teach and model how to navigate the complex landscape of information. Teachers must acknowledge that individuals perceive and understand events in a variety of ways based on their lived experiences. Furthermore, this assignment provides a perfect opportunity to have an ongoing conversation about media literacy—specifically, the concepts of bias and the importance of evaluating reliable sources. With most students getting their news from social media and video platforms, teaching them how to process information from various perspectives in a safe and respectful environment is a foundational skill for civic life.

Fostering Student Agency and Empathy

Flexibility is a cornerstone of this assignment. If a student is passionate about a different topic, they should be welcome to clear it with you. The primary objective is for students to engage with the news, and allowing them to explore a topic that is personally meaningful or fascinating can significantly boost their interest. This flexibility also creates space for students to make connections to their own unique backgrounds or lived experiences. You can also consider occasionally giving a "free choice" option where students can choose what they are interested in, but be prepared to give some suggestions for students who might be stumped or feel overwhelmed by all the options.

It's also important to be mindful of students' diverse backgrounds. Sometimes a student's aversion to a particular topic may be a sign of a trauma response, and a flexible, respectful approach is necessary. For unforeseen events, like an earthquake or hurricane, offer students the choice between the original weekly topic and the new, unfolding event. This adaptability demonstrates the dynamic nature of history and provides a real-time lesson in its impact. Events don't happen on a straight timeline; multiple events can happen simultaneously. Giving students the ability to navigate this landscape will help them to become more flexible and thoughtful citizens themselves.

Engaging the Wider Community

Finally, extend the learning beyond the classroom by involving parents and guardians. A simple but effective tip is to tell parents that they can always ask their kids what the current event for the week is. This not only encourages a family conversation about the news but also reinforces the importance of staying informed and makes civic discussion a part of students' home lives.

It's important to have an ongoing conversation about media bias and reliable sources for information. Most students are getting their news from social media or videos. We will talk more about this in the *Skills of Critical Thinking* section.

Here are some examples of ways to highlight the skill ***Current Events Analysis*** *in your classroom*

- A student can read two contrasting news articles on a current political issue and articulate the different viewpoints presented and potential biases.
- Students can take a current event and evaluate parallels between the current event and a historical event.

- Students can research a current event in another country and analyze the governmental response to the event.
- Students can identify a current event that may represent an overarching theme that may connect events in either other locations or in the United States throughout history.
- Students can craft a claims–evidence–reasoning prompt to engage others in understanding this current event more thoroughly.
- A student can teach the background of the current event to the class if it is something with which they have particular knowledge or interest in learning more about.
- Students can compose headlines about the event that represent different viewpoints.

Time to Reflect: *How can we best connect current events to historical events or students' knowledge of government? How might it be useful for your students to connect with their knowledge of other countries or parts of the world?*

Skill CK5. Civic Engagement Preparedness: *I can identify and explain various pathways for civic participation and advocacy, explaining how individuals can contribute to their communities and larger society.*

The idea of getting high school students to proactively engage in their communities is often a daunting one. However, while it's a challenge to get them to initiate on their own, many are enthusiastic participants when opportunities are presented. The key is to prepare them for civic engagement by demystifying the process and providing accessible pathways to action.

As educators, we are uniquely positioned to serve as catalysts for this preparation. In many communities across America, schools are not only the largest gathering of people in a single place on any given day, but also the epicenter of rich thinking, creative endeavors, and collaboration. The following suggestions are designed to leverage this unique position in anticipation of more formal "action civics" projects.

Know Your Community's Landscape

Begin by truly taking stock of the community around you. This involves going beyond a cursory glance to identify both its strengths and its challenges. Engaging your class in this ongoing process of observation helps students see their community not just as a backdrop for their lives, but as a dynamic system in which they have a role to play.

Bring the Community to Your Classroom

There are people in your community doing amazing things, and they can serve as powerful role models for your students. Welcome community leaders—such as local politicians, non-profit organizers, or civic volunteers—to speak to your class about their work. Even if an in-person visit isn't possible, a virtual call via Zoom can be an equally impactful experience. Prioritize leaders who may provide a sense of connection with your students, whether through shared language, diverse backgrounds, or similar lived experiences. These interactions help students see that civic participation is not an abstract concept but a real-world activity carried out by people just like them.

Leverage Existing School Partnerships

Your school may already have a robust network of community partnerships through its various clubs and teams. Explore what these groups are doing and look for ways your class can support them. Can your students design a new website for the school's service club? Can they organize a fundraiser for the athletics team's community charity drive? Conversely, if a group of students is looking for a way to make a difference and you are in a position to help, supporting the establishment of a new club can foster a strong sense of belonging, leadership, and civic pride.

Empower Students to Make Their Voices Heard

One of the most fundamental acts of civic participation is communicating with one's representatives, yet students often don't know what to say or how to say it. Consider a project where students write an essay on a topic connected to their communities and then teach them how to transform that essay into a formal letter to their elected official. This is also an opportunity to teach students about the nuances of language—such as formality and persuasive techniques—as they craft their messages. As a practical and often-overlooked lesson, actually show them how to properly address an envelope. This simple act demystifies the process and can only help them down the road!

The ultimate goal of these activities is to prepare students to be active citizens. By providing them with a clear understanding of the pathways for civic participation, you are empowering them to contribute to their communities and larger society.

Once students get introduced to the various avenues and people who make an impact, and ways that they fit into local, state, and national government, it's time for them to start looking at their communities more critically and see what can—and should—get fixed. The next chapter helps them to take action in their communities.

Time to Reflect: *What do you know about the community in which you teach in terms of history, people who live there, current challenges, or local government? What do you know about community members, their languages, their religions, and what is important to them? How do these two parts of the fabrics of our communities intersect?*

Spotlight on Sources

Bill of Rights Institute: https://billofrightsinstitute.org/ A comprehensive set of civics lessons.

Civics Renewal Network: https://www.civicsrenewalnetwork.org/ Over 40 organizations, with hundreds of resources for teaching civics.

Street Law: https://streetlaw.org/ They turn Supreme Court Cases into powerful classroom lessons.

Icivics: https://vision.icivics.org/ Lessons and interactive video games.

270towin: https://www.270towin.com/ Interactive Electoral College Map

References

Annenberg Public Policy Center. (2022). *Americans' Civics Knowledge Drops on First Amendment and Branches of Government*. University of Pennsylvania.

Locke, J. (2009). *Second Treatise of Government* (J. Gough, Ed.). Blackwell Publishing. (Original work published 1689)

Merriam-Webster, Incorporated. (n.d.). *Merriam-Webster.com dictionary*. Retrieved November 23, 2025, from https://www.merriam-webster.com/

Niemöller, M. (1946). *First They Came* (Retrieved version). United States Holocaust Memorial Museum. Retrieved November 22, 2025, from https://www.ushmm.org/wlc/en/article.php?ModuleId=10007392

Pew Research Center. (2023, September 19). Highly negative views of American politics. https://www.pewresearch.org/politics/2023/09/19/americans-dismal-views-of-the-nations-politics/

5

Community Engagement

Addressing Root Causes of Injustice

We often teach civics at a national level, but we come up short when it comes to the local issues. This creates a disconnect, leaving students unaware of the very communities that shape them. Shouldn't they know who their local legislators are, or who serves on their school board, in addition to knowing the president? Shouldn't they have the chance to shape their community, just as it has shaped them? At the local level is where citizens may see the actual fruits of their labor, feel the effects of their advocacy, and hear the echoes of their voices. This is where the government is run by their neighbors and community members and they may actually know the people who are making the decisions.

Across the country, schools are often the biggest collection of people and a hub of energy, creativity, and hard work. Yet, they've become increasingly isolated from the communities that surround them. Because of safety concerns, schools and communities have stopped working together, but unfortunately it has created a chasm between students and their communities.

The best way to bridge this gap is to put schools back in the center of the community by actively cultivating community engagement. One of the most effective methods for this is through action civics projects. These projects allow students

DOI: 10.4324/9781003746614-5

to really examine their communities, determine root causes of problems and injustice, and seek out solutions. Along the way they will create connections with leaders and changemakers in their communities, putting schools back on the radar of decision-makers and advocacy back on the radars of the schools.

> Schools do an excellent job focusing on academics, but civic engagement often receives less emphasis. To build stronger connections between schools and communities, learning should extend beyond the classroom walls. This doesn't just mean field trips for entertainment, but meaningful, hands-on experiences: planting a community garden to understand local ecology, visiting museums to see how history and culture are preserved, or observing a court session to witness civic processes in action. These kinds of activities show students how communities function and allow them to participate in that process. When students consistently and authentically interact with their community, they not only deepen their learning but also develop a stronger sense of civic responsibility and engagement.
>
> —Kaitlyn, adjunct history professor

Imagine a community garden tended by students, a cemetery cleanup, or a welcome video for newcomers created in their own language(s). These aren't just projects; they are powerful examples of students addressing public problems and strengthening their communities. As the C3 Framework from NCSS states, "People demonstrate civic engagement when they address public problems individually and collaboratively and when they maintain, strengthen, and improve communities and societies" (NCSS, 2013, p. 31). In addition to the benefits for the community, the sense of pride, belonging, and ownership that students feel when engaging in an initiative like this is immeasurable.

This chapter will empower you to empower your students. You'll find step-by-step guidelines for leading students through the process of community engagement: from assessing local needs and challenges to researching and collaborating with community partners, creating an action plan, taking action, and reflecting on their work. You will be encouraging them along the way and redirecting them if they need to pivot to a slightly different angle of their topic. Not only will you look at action civics in a new way, you will also consider different points of access for advocacy and activism to build these skills in yourself and your students.

SEL connection: Considering the different perspectives and situations of your students' families is important. Not all families or community members feel that they have a voice in the community or local government for a variety of reasons. True discourse and reflections on the perception of advocacy and empowerment are necessary to understand interactions and interconnectedness of different stakeholders.

Some may say that this is not supported by the district curriculum. However, the connections to social studies are clear and there may be connections to language arts, math, science, and other related courses as well. Collaboration across curricula and departments will empower the school community in ways that will surprise everyone.

This may feel like a daunting task, but a helpful way to think about it is to see yourself as a guide or a midwife, not a project manager. Students will do the research, identify problems, connect with community members, and take action. Your job is to provide structure, guidance, and a listening ear. While it may be tempting to step in and solve problems for them, resist the urge. This is where the most valuable learning happens. They will face setbacks and frustrations, and that's exactly what prepares them for real life.

As Nelson Mandela wisely said, "It always seems impossible until it's done."

> **Time to Reflect:** *What reservations do you have about action civics projects and how to empower students to take action? What obstacles do you think may be challenging as you begin to roll out these projects? Who may be stakeholders in the school and community who can be support systems in a variety of ways?*

The Second Competency: Community Engagement

Community Engagement: The learner participates in community life, problem-solving, and advocacy for positive change, and then takes action to create the change.

Associated Skills

To achieve this competency, students will develop a range of skills (Table 5.1):

TABLE 5.1 Skills of Community Engagement

CE1	**Community needs identification and analysis** I can assess my local community to identify unmet needs, potential challenges, root causes, existing assets and the impact of these issues on members of the community.
CE2	**Collaborative problem-solving and planning** I can collaborate with community stakeholders to brainstorm solutions to identified community problems, and create an action plan that takes diverse perspectives and available resources into consideration.
CE3	**Advocacy and persuasive communication** I can research and design a positive change with evidence-based examples and advocate for this change with the relevant audience to make it possible.
CE4	**Action implementation** I can actively participate and contribute to initiatives designed to address identified community needs.
CE5	**Showcase, reflection and impact assessment** I can showcase my results to classmates and community members, and reflect upon the process of community action, the impact of my efforts, and my growth as a citizen.

Key Vocabulary from Merriam-Webster (n.d.)

- **Community Engagement:** *active participation of an individual in their community's life, including problem-solving and advocacy.*
- **Advocacy:** *promoting positive change by researching, designing, and providing evidence-based examples to a relevant audience.*
- **Community Stakeholder:** *a member of the community who has a vested interest in the community and its needs, including residents and those who work there or legislate on behalf of that group of people.*
- **Needs Assessment:** *identifying unmet needs, potential challenges and existing assets (as well as stakeholders) within a community.*
- **Root Cause:** *the fundamental underlying reason why there is a problem or issue in a community.*
- **Showcase:** *a special event designed to publicly display and celebrate student achievement or skills.*

Skill CE1: Community Needs Identification and Analysis: *I can assess my local community to identify unmet needs, potential challenges, existing assets and the impact of these issues on members of the community.*

Exploring Our Identities First

Before we can begin to explore the complex web of our communities, it's a good idea to have students explore who they are and what makes them unique. This may bring up different feelings among students, some of them really love examining themselves and some students would rather do anything than examine their lives. By first reflecting on who you are, where you come from, what you care about, and what you dream for the future, you're able to then look at the community around you, that shaped you, and assess it more objectively.

There are lots of ways to have students examine their identities, but also their beliefs.

- **Identity Maps:** Identity maps are a good way for students to write down who they are and where they come from. Have students start with a circle in the center of a paper, and then write their name in it. Then radiating out from the circle in lines are the things that "identify" them. This could be ways that they identify themselves as "daughter" or "student" or ways that other people would describe them as "shy" or "funny." You can make variations like replacing the circle in the center with a heart of a star, or have students create a pie chart of themselves instead.
- **I Believe:** In addition to the Identity Maps, you can also teach a class on beliefs. It's important at the outset to distinguish an opinion (a personal thought, judgment or opinion) and a belief (a deeply held conviction that is based on morals, values, or worldview.) Based on the "This I Believe" series from NPR (https://www.npr.org/series/4538138/this-i-believe), you can begin the class with a series of belief statements and have students literally get up and place themselves along a line in the room that has "Strongly Agree" on one side, "Strongly Disagree" on the other side, and "Neutral" in the middle. Here are some examples of "I believe" statements you can use:

    - I believe that social media shows a person's highlight reel, not their full story.
    - I believe it's more important to be kind than to be right.
    - I believe that a person's character is more important than their academic achievements.
    - I believe it's okay to change your mind about your friends, your interests, or your future.
    - I believe that failure is a necessary part of growth.
    - I believe that it's important to advocate for yourself, even when it's uncomfortable.
    - I believe that having a few close friends is better than being popular.

After the exercise where students are up and moving, transition to desk work by having them listen to an essay from the NPR archives. Then have your students choose a belief and write a short essay. You may want to give them an example from your own life. For an added challenge, you can have the students read their essays and record them, and then send their recordings for grading.

SEL connection: It is essential to engage students in reflecting upon things that are integral to who they are and what they believe. However, educators must be culturally responsive to those for whom this type of activity may be a difficult or triggering exercise. Some may be struggling with understanding different aspects of their identities or belief systems. Students who have experienced trauma or difficulties in their past, related to their families, or who are currently dealing with challenges may be reluctant to participate in activities in which they feel uncomfortable. Having alternate activities—even if they are reflecting on the identity of a famous person instead of themselves—shows students that they do not have to "push through" when they feel uneasy and there are other ways that they can fully participate.

As educators, it is important to collaborate with other professionals in both the district (counselor, nurse) and the community (local support services) as a first step in supporting our students' varied needs.

Next Explore Our Communities

Now that students have a good grounding in who they are and what they believe, they can turn their gaze to the world around them. At this point they are not providing solutions, they are just coming up with problems as they observe them. This may seem like a very surface-level activity, but this type of analysis of one's world, community, or home may be very eye-opening. There are things that people just accept as "the way it is" and do not ever notice them until a project such as this.

Here are some examples of ways to highlight the skill ***Community Needs Identification and Analysis*** *in your classroom:*

- **Problem Gallery Walk:** A great way to help students brainstorm problems is to set up a Problem Gallery Walk. Post five large pieces of chart paper around the room and label each one with a different topic: **School**, **Town**, **State**, **Nation**, and **World**. Give students a marker and have them walk to each chart, writing down one or more problems, unmet needs, or potential challenges they see for each area. After everyone has had a chance to brainstorm, have students do a second gallery walk. This time, they should place a check mark next to any problem they agree with or feel is important. Students can note if there may be other perspectives regarding this problem. Finally, ask each student to review the checked problems and write down the three they are most interested in exploring further.
- **Trees and Root Causes:** Once students have chosen three problems they want to explore, it's time to dig deeper with an arts-and-crafts activity. Have each student choose one problem and create a Root Causes Tree. The trunk of the tree (above ground) is the visible problem itself. The roots (below ground) represent the causes of the problem. Encourage students to think deeply and ask "Why?" to get to the root of the issue. For example, "Why are people not getting enough to eat?" might lead to causes like poverty, food deserts, or lack of education about nutrition. The branches can represent the results or consequences of the problem. This activity helps students visualize the complex nature of a problem, showing that what we see on the surface is often supported by deeper, interconnected issues. Extensions may include brainstorming things people can do at the local, state, and national level to address different parts of this problem or writing letters to stakeholders or legislators to bring attention to the issues (Figure 5.1).

FIGURE 5.1 Trees drawn by students.

Root Causes Trees

Tip of the Iceberg: This activity is a great alternative to the Root Causes Tree, especially for certain problems. Have students draw an iceberg, with the water line clearly marked. The tip of the iceberg (above the water) is the visible problem itself. The larger portion of the iceberg (below the water) represents the underlying causes of the problem. Like the tree activity, the Iceberg Model helps students think past the surface-level issue. The key difference is that this model focuses exclusively on the relationship between the problem and its root causes, making it a powerful tool for analyzing a single issue without also exploring its consequences. You can present both models to students and let them choose the one that best fits the problem they are exploring. Students can reflect on the potential misconceptions of people who may only see the problem for what is immediately visible and how they can engage community members in looking more deeply to see the whole picture.

Conferencing Is Key

As students are working, it's essential to circulate and conference with each group. After everyone is settled, let them know when you will begin your check-ins. When you sit down with a group, give them your full attention. Listen to their ideas and concerns and provide thoughtful feedback. BEST practice note: Providing a shared document or written notes of your feedback may be helpful for students who need a chance to process and would like to refer back to your suggestions. This may be in a shared document, through sticky notes (with pictures taken), or within a shared notebook. This type of documentation provides a consistent way that you can assess growth and collaboratively work with your students in individual and unique ways.

Conferencing is a great way to connect with your students as a support system in their work. Making this a regular part of your class routine shows students that you are a resource and that their ideas are valued. It puts them in the driver's seat of their own learning, while also ensuring that you stay connected to their progress. Ensuring that each student contributes to the conferencing is essential and provides the framework for the importance of everyone's individual contribution to the team effort. This consistent interaction also reinforces that every student's voice matters and that they can't simply "skate by" unnoticed. Everyone's voices are valued and necessary.

> I learned a lot about elections and voting. Town elections are much less popular than presidential elections, with only 11% of registered voters voting in the last Mendon town election. I learned the best ways to teach young children about voting without making it political as well. I also learned how to talk to professional people and how to orchestrate events and contests. —Student reflection, when asked, "What did you learn from the civics project or from the civics project process?"

A Time for Modeling and Creativity

Before students begin, it's crucial to model your expectations. Show them an example of both a Root Causes Tree and a Tip of the Iceberg model. This is likely a new concept for them, and some students may find it difficult to grasp. BEST practices note: As this may be something different than anything your students have done before, this type of explicit modeling may ease feelings of uncertainty in terms of expectations. Modeling should include the relevant languaging that students will use as well as how to use scaffolds as necessary. It is also important to stress that models are just that: an example. If students feel that they best think in a different way or express themselves through some other channel or modality, that is amazing.

A great way to model this is by doing a "think aloud" for a problem. Walk them through your thought process: *Why do you think this is a problem? What are the immediate effects? What are the deeper causes? Who may be stakeholders in working through this problem and who would benefit from it?* Demonstrate where each part of the problem fits on the chosen model. Not only does this model the process that one may take in this part of an action civics project, but it also models the act of planning and the vocabulary that may be useful. It is important that all students have these opportunities to dig deeper into the content while having access to relevant scaffolds as needed. Some may include sentence stems or frames, graphic organizers, or potential links to resources that may clarify the problem.

Recognize that not all students are comfortable with art. You can have a few **templates** of the tree and iceberg ready for those who might prefer a structured approach. Encourage everyone to **color** their final work and make it their own. If students choose to represent these concepts through a different visual, this may be another way they can engage in creatively analyzing these problems. Observing and analyzing complex social issues can be mentally taxing, so combining this critical thinking with a creative outlet can make the process more enjoyable and less overwhelming.

BEST Practices to Meet Diverse Needs of Learners

- **Bridge** (English/multilingual learners): Short videos, with subtitles if possible, designed to build schema on the background of the problem are helpful. Key vocabulary that is connected to the problem is frontloaded and discussed in context. Roles within the community are defined and students are encouraged to make connections with their own possible prior knowledge of local governments.
- **Expand** (gifted students): Students may take charge of establishing additional stakeholders' contributions beyond the project and how the project may build and be sustainable even after this portion is completed.
- **Support** (students with learning challenges or differences): Providing various options for students to complete these assignments (some may have lower language demands, others may use electronic ways to create visuals, audio commentary instead of writing extensively, etc.) may lessen potential confusion and allow for students to work in their areas of strength. Rubrics may be clarified and made into a checklist.
- **Teamwork:** Students may work collaboratively to "talk out" the different perspectives regarding a problem that has been identified. The key is to understand that all points of view have reasoning behind them and examining the reasoning (even if we may disagree) is essential

to fully analyze all sides. Students can chart the varying perspectives with supporting details while also indicating potential results or consequences.

Skill CE2. Collaborative Problem-Solving and Planning: *I can collaborate with community stakeholders to brainstorm solutions to identified community problems, and create an action plan that takes diverse perspectives and available resources into consideration.*

Choosing a "Dragon" to Slay

After students have identified problems in their community, the next step is for them to choose a way to address those issues. How you approach this depends on the age of your students and the time you have to devote to the project.

For younger students or when time is limited, a single, whole-class project may be the most effective approach. This is especially helpful if it would be difficult for students to transport themselves or communicate with community leaders. For older students or a class with more time, you might consider having them work in small groups on different projects. Both methods can provide powerful learning experiences.

The Massachusetts Department of Elementary and Secondary Education has provided a great guide that helps you to think about the size and scope of your project (Table 5.2).

A Word About Community

Before students choose their projects, it's essential to define what "community" means to them. A helpful way to think about this is through a concentric circles model: with the School at the center, surrounded by the Town, then the State, the Nation, and, finally, the World.

Depending on their background and how long they have been in the area, a student might consider their community to be as small as the school itself, or even a subset like a club or a sports team. A student who has recently arrived might not

TABLE 5.2 Factors to Consider for Action Civics Projects

Size	*Benefits*	*Limitations*
Individual	♦ Student autonomy and aligned to personal interest and identity ♦ Project can be tailored to meet needs of students ♦ Students tend to be most motivated to complete a topic that is connected their personal interest	♦ Less opportunity for collaboration and consensus-building ♦ Hands-on support is more individualized ♦ Students and teachers may be overwhelmed without a clear process for taking action
Small Group	♦ Groups can be made based on topics ♦ Group topics across class or classes to share resources and streamline ♦ Opportunity for collaboration ♦ Hands-on support from teacher in conferencing. Setting goals, facilitating connections is streamlined	♦ Consensus takes time ♦ Instruction on norms and collaboration necessary ♦ Still can be many topics and contacts for teachers
Whole Class	♦ Teachers can focus energy around one topic, especially if they have many classes with projects ♦ Teachers can take more active role in connecting students with resources and developing an action ♦ Groups within the whole class can choose different actions	♦ Consensus takes time and students may not be as invested in the chosen topic ♦ Teachers need to create and structure tasks to engage all students

(Massachusetts Department of Elementary and Secondary Education, 2019)

yet feel connected enough to create change at the town or state level. For them, a project focused on the school can be a powerful choice, as their "new eyes" might spot injustices that others no longer see.

> I had newcomer students who were not well connected in the community and who did not speak English well as part of my class that did civics projects. They chose to tackle an injustice that they experienced when they arrived at the school, namely, that there was nothing written in their language to tell them what anything was. They opted to create welcome videos in three different foreign languages that showed the next newcomers what to expect in the school, how to get around the building, and what the school culture was like. That was two years ago, but we still use those videos today.
>
> —Anonymous teacher

Sometimes community is used in a fashion that excludes certain groups of people—particularly during times of potential transition—and this is something about which educators must be aware. If there is a sense of division within the community members in the classroom, it is absolutely essential that the teacher addresses this issue with firm kindness and compassion—but no tolerance for marginalizing anyone in the classroom or community by "othering" them.

Choosing Is Hard

Students can get really excited when they're able to choose a topic and a problem they've researched, and they feel confident moving forward. More often, though, students are presented with a few choices and aren't sure which problem to address. Conferencing with them can help, as you talk through what they like about a topic and what they think they might be able to accomplish. This will help them decide. Some students might know the problem but be unsure of what to do about it. By being a good listener and helping them see what's possible, you can help them choose a path forward. They might even ask for a nudge, "What do you think I should do?" If that happens, it's a good idea to guide them toward a project with the highest likelihood of success, based on the student, the problem, and the amount of time you have.

> **Time to Reflect:** *What resources are you aware of that can help your students succeed in this endeavor? How can you be sure that they are using reliable sources? How may you engage peers or community members in discourse around sources and topics?*

Building a Foundation of Support

Action civics projects are a big commitment, and their success often hinges on support from school administrators, teachers, and other staff. To get that buy-in, be clear with your school about your goals and what you need from them. Also effectively communicating the benefits of these projects for both the students and the community is essential.

For example, when your students begin their in-depth research, ask your school librarian for help. They can give a presentation on proper research methods, perhaps with a slideshow students can reference later. Having students learn to find peer-reviewed articles and explore the resources available in the library or media center will greatly improve their research skills. This collaboration also builds a valuable connection between students and staff, providing an additional point of contact for help.

How much research should students do? That's up to you, but remember the information isn't just coming from sources in the library, but also from people in the community, legislators, and possibly surveys developed by the students. Let's look at those more in depth.

To gain a comprehensive understanding of the issue, students should be collecting different types of information to answer these basic questions:

- **What is the current situation?** This includes data and personal accounts of the issue.
- **Why does this happen?** The need to uncover the systemic root causes.
- **How can students address it?** Identifying potential solutions through policy or sweat equity.
- **Who can help?** This involves identifying key stakeholders and targets who can support the solutions.
- **How will students determine or measure success?** In order to connect the goals with data and research, students can identify key outcomes that may indicate that they have moved towards positive engagement.

Walking Alongside Community Members

Engaging with community members is one of the most valuable things you can do to help students connect with their community. The wealth of information held by these individuals—many of whom students have never met—can be transformative. Students often exist in a silo, primarily interacting with their own age group and their parents' generation. The daily routine of school, activities, homework, and family dinner creates a significant divide, particularly between young people and senior citizens. This gap, however, can be bridged during the research phase of an action civics project.

To facilitate this, have students answer the following questions:

- **Identify contacts:** Who in the community is connected to your problem? This could be a local official, a nonprofit leader, a business owner, or a concerned neighbor. Have students write down their names, titles, workplaces, phone numbers, and email addresses.
- **Reach out:** Students should contact 2–3 community members by email or phone. In their communication, they should clearly state who they are, what their project is, and what they hope to learn. Remind them to be

respectful of the person's time and to express gratitude for their help.

- **Conduct an interview:** Students should prepare a few questions in advance. They need to listen carefully, take notes, and ask follow-up questions to gain a deeper understanding.
- **Reflect:** After their conversations, students should write down what they learned. Did the person's story or perspective change their understanding of the problem?

Before students send an email, it's a good idea for them to draft it and review it with you to check for grammar and spelling. It's also important that they always copy you on their emails to ensure that all interactions remain positive and cooperative and that an adult is monitoring all communications between the students and community members. These emails should follow a professional format and you may have to provide templates or samples for them to follow.

Similarly, since most students no longer use the phone for conversations, they may feel awkward speaking with an adult on the phone. Consider having them write a script for what they plan to say and practice the conversation with you *before they actually make the call.*

Time to Reflect: *Do you have a network of community members that you already interact with for other reasons or events? Are there community organizations (scouts, nonprofits) that would benefit from the projects? Are there local grants that may support the work? Before beginning this project with your students, who else could you contact that you know would be a helpful resource to your students?*

A Jury of Your Peers

Sometimes, the best way to understand an issue is to hear directly from your peers. A survey can be a powerful tool for this, especially if the problem is connected to the lives of teenagers, like mental health, bullying, or pressures connected to college admissions or social media. To facilitate this, you can have students create surveys and have other students answer the questions. They can even create QR codes to have other students directly connect and answer the questions online.

Here is a set of instructions for your students to help them to create their own surveys for their peers:

- **Craft your survey**. If you decide to create a survey, make sure your questions are clear, neutral, and directly related to your problem. Avoid leading questions.
- **Get the teacher's approval**. Don't skip this step.
- **Share with your peers**. Distribute your survey and collect responses.
- **Analyze the results**. Review the data you collected. What patterns or trends do you see? What did your peers' responses tell you about the problem?

Preparation is key, and it's important to review the questions your students want to ask, ensure their neutrality, and safeguard the anonymity of the students answering the survey. If you are in doubt, consider asking your guidance counselor if the questions the students want to ask are appropriate, respectful, and relevant.

Legislators

If students need to reach out to their legislators, a lot of the rules above still apply, writing a script would help, as well as defining the best way to respond to them. Oftentimes state and federal legislators have a portal that is read by staff. Explain to students that they may get a form letter and then further contact later down the road. You may be surprised at the response students get from their legislators. Politicians love photo opportunities with students!

Consider making a document as a "catch-all" for your students, where they can place their articles, contacts, rough drafts of phone call scripts and/or email templates. Letting them have it all in one place helps them to develop a big picture on the scope of the problem, the help they can muster, and the direction of the plan.

> **Time to Reflect:** *Once students create these contacts, how can you maximize these connections with local stakeholders? In what ways can students leverage their language and literacy skills to engage others?*

Skill CE3. Advocacy and Persuasive Communication: *I can research and design a positive change with evidence-based examples and advocate for this change with the relevant audience to make it possible.*

Project Preparation

After students have conducted their research—by reading articles, interviewing community experts, surveying their peers, and contacting legislators—they are ready to create an action plan they can achieve within the time allotted. This is the perfect time for each group to formally declare their project and get feedback from their classmates.

To prepare for this, have students complete a simple document with a few clear, concise sentences about their project. The document should include:

- **Civics Project Topic/Title**
- **Name(s) of Student(s)**
- **Summary of Project**
- **Root Cause**
- **Goals of the Project**

Next, have them practice a short "elevator pitch" of their project. Presentations should be brief, lasting no more than 2–3 minutes, so they'll need to focus and refine their message. This type of activity provides opportunities to focus on persuasive speech, considering the audience, and analyzing/prioritizing information in a way that aligns with critical thinking.

Peer Review and Presentation

Now, it's time for the peer-review process, which is a powerful first step in persuasive communication. Students will present their proposals to their classmates. You can even consider having them present to another class to broaden their audience. As they listen, their peers should be given a few sticky notes to write down the strengths of each proposal and any questions they have.

After a group presents, their peers will give them the sticky notes to attach to the back of their project document. This might feel a bit chaotic, but it's a low-stakes way for students to practice their persuasion skills and for their peers to critically analyze the messages they receive. Have each group present no more than three times to different classmates to give them ample practice.

Reflection and Revision

Once students are back in their seats, have them remove the sticky notes and sort them into two categories: "positive comments" and "room for improvement." This is a crucial moment for reflection and revision. If they received similar feedback—for example, that the root cause was unclear—they can adjust their proposal accordingly.

This process is a two-way street: presenters learn how to accept constructive criticism, and their peers learn how to give it effectively. Students should then take their initial document and mark it up with anything they want to add, subtract, or change.

Finally, give them a new copy of the same document, this time with a space at the end for reflection. Ask them to consider the following questions, which will result in productive and honest answers:

- **Accomplishments:** What do I feel good about accomplishing today?
- **Challenges:** What still needs work?
- **Concerns:** What's my biggest concern?

This exercise is going to feel chaotic; you're going to have a lot of things happening simultaneously, but it's beneficial for students to do this work with their peers and not necessarily with you watching. To quote a teacher that does this lesson, "We're throwing them into the deep end of the pool" with this exercise. Allowing them to hone their message, their goals, and their underlying root cause will set them up for success when they need to contact community members about their project once it begins to happen.

Time to Reflect: *Do you have a colleague who would lend their students to listen to your students' proposals, or can you partner up with a class that is doing the same action civics project and listen to each other's proposals? Are there colleagues who would volunteer to be mentors for your students? Do you need to notify your administrators if you're going to a third space (like a hallway or library) to accomplish this?*

Skill CE4. Action Implementation: *I can actively participate and contribute to initiatives designed to address identified community needs.*

Taking Action

This is the phase where students take their ideas from the page and bring them to life. While they'll be writing their action plan and setting out to accomplish it, the real learning happens when they encounter the inevitable roadblocks. Projects rarely go from A to B in a straight line, and this step is designed to help students manage their time and be adaptable.

When students create their action plan, it might look something like this list for a community garden project:

1. Find a piece of land that would be right for a community garden.
2. Contact the school/town hall/community club about permission to build the garden.
3. Raise funds for plants by having a bake sale.

4. Buy plants from local garden center.
5. Make the beds and plant the garden.
6. Create educational material to provide the public about the use of the community garden.
7. Coordinate with the local gardening club about upkeep and future plants.
8. Create a poster about the garden.
9. Present at the Showcase.
10. Reflect on the experience.

The key lesson here is learning how to be proactive when a project stalls. Students are used to getting immediate responses, but a call to a community board member or a municipal employee might not be returned for a few days. Instead of stopping everything while they wait, they can look at their action plan and find another task to work on.

We saw this happen with a community garden project that got delayed by a cold spring. The local garden center wouldn't sell the plants until they were in bloom, and it rained every Saturday of the month. The students didn't let this stop them. While they were waiting for the plants and the sun, they got a head-start on their poster presentation and educational materials. This kept the project moving forward and taught them how to navigate real-world timelines.

Have students write a running record on what they are doing, and have them upload (if online) or staple) if on paper proof of their work.

> At my school, inevitably, one student asks the same question every year, "You mean, we actually have to DO this?" As a result, my department calls the Action Implementation step "The Do Step" and teachers will ask their students, "What is your DO?" meaning, what is it they are going to accomplish, and prove that they've accomplished it?
>
> —Darcy

The Power of the Pivot

Sometimes, no matter how much a student researches and plans, their project idea just won't work out. It could be that the idea has already been done, or a different group is already in the process of doing it. This is where the power of the pivot comes in. Learning to adapt is a crucial skill for any project.

Consider the students who wanted to bring electric car charging stations to their school. They did thorough research, spoke with a vendor, and even identified a location in the parking lot. But when they presented their plan to the superintendent's office, they found out the school already had a charging station project in the works with a different vendor. Instead of giving up, the students pivoted. They launched an educational campaign for the school and community about the benefits of the new charging stations, creating posters and giving presentations to local groups.

In another case, a student passionate about housing insecurity planned to work with Habitat for Humanity. He learned about the issue, connected with the local chapter's director, and was ready to volunteer. He then discovered that he had to be 18 to work on the build sites. His solution? He created a fundraiser for the organization, turning his disappointment into a positive contribution.

These examples show that a project doesn't have to end just because the original plan hits a dead end. Instead, students can use their creativity and research to find a new, meaningful way to achieve their goals.

Real-World Problems

One of the most unexpected challenges students might face is not with their project, but with the people they need to work with. They might try to connect with someone who is on maternity leave, or discover a key position is currently vacant. They could even find themselves in the middle of a historic feud or a long-held rivalry between two organizations.

These are "real-world" problems that adults deal with regularly but are often brand new for students. You can't prepare them for every possible interpersonal challenge, but you can help them learn to handle them when they arise.

This is exactly why continued conferencing with your students is so important. By meeting with them regularly, you can advise them on how to navigate these sticky situations, helping them develop valuable communication and problem-solving skills that go far beyond their project.

Skill CE5. Showcase, Reflection and Impact Assessment: I can showcase my results to classmates and community members, and reflect upon the process of community action, the impact of my efforts, and my growth as a citizen.

The Showcase

The final step is for students to showcase their results! A successful showcase requires careful planning, both for the event itself and for student preparation.

On your end, you'll need to reserve a space and time, coordinate with administration, and send out invitations to parents, community partners, and local media. To make the day go smoothly, consider coordinating with other school departments to establish a common set of rules for the event, including things like dress code and food/drink policies. This helps set clear expectations and reduces student stress.

For the students, the showcase is their chance to shine. They should create a trifold display that clearly explains their project: the problem they tackled, their research (including any data or graphs), the solution they implemented, and the results they achieved. It's important to remind them that the trifold is simply an aid; they should be prepared to explain their project directly to classmates and community members. To ensure they are ready, have them practice their **presentation** in advance (Figure 5.2).

On the day of the event, students should arrive early to set up. You can simplify this process by assigning students to numbered tables and providing a map for guests. To avoid overcrowding, consider setting aside a specific time for students to walk around and see one another's projects. Finally, to provide students with valuable feedback, have paper or digital feedback forms available for visitors. This allows guests to share their thoughts and provides students with a record of their success.

Students will rise to the occasion, but expect some jitters, especially if this is the first time that they are presenting to

FIGURE 5.2 Civics Showcase at Nipmuc Regional High School in Upton, MA.

people other than their classmates. As this is a high-impact way to engage in public speaking in small groups, students have the opportunity to connect with members of the community in a different way (Figure 5.3).

> **SEL connection:** Some of your students may have difficulty in presenting for whatever reason and we provide different ways for them to actively engage if they are unable to present in a traditional fashion. Students may record short bits of information and can play it when community members come around. Students may partner with a peer leader or student who is not currently taking this class to engage in scripted "interviews" in which the peer asks questions for the student to answer (using notes or whatever other supports needed). Students may do this project in any language with signage that indicates which language. Students may also use visuals that explain their project without a speech.
>
> Please note that community members must be aware that not all students may be presenting in the same way.

FIGURE 5.3 Student showcasing their project helping children in hospitals deal with loss and the process of mourning.

Reflection

Your students have done so much work to make this a reality. They should take some real time to reflect on their experiences. Their responses will surprise and delight you. Among the questions you can ask them are:

- What did you learn about yourself during this project?
- What do you wish you had done sooner?
- What is something you enjoyed while working on this project?
- Who was the most useful contact and why?
- What are ways that this project could be improved?
- If you had one wish for this project what would it be?
- What do you believe was the impact of your project?
- How has this project helped you to grow as a citizen?

Also consider asking your students if their project is something that could be carried on in future years, and how that could happen. These are called **legacy projects** and they are multi-year, multi-cohort projects that get handed off from one generation to another (Daniels et al., 2025). These projects could be an idea that only just got going, or a good partnership with a community member that would be beneficial to continue.

Portrait of a civic pioneer: In the winter of 2017 one of my students came to me with a proposal. Our class had just begun to brainstorm for what would become a semester-long action civics project. We were in search of a community issue that we could devote months to addressing—and one of my students, Rebecca, a Congolese refugee and high school junior, had an idea. She had noticed how some classmates, some friends were hungry and didn't have enough food at home. Might this be our focus? Rebecca was intimately familiar with food insecurity. She was born and raised in an Ugandan refugee camp near the border of the Democratic Republic of the Congo, her parents' home until war forced them to flee. As she would share publicly a year later,"In our refugee camp, life was not easy, but we had no other option…I was often very sick. But I learned that if I worked hard and focused on my education I could get better and could make positive changes in my life." In our class, Rebecca was bubbly, confident, and endlessly generous. In little time her classmates had coalesced around her idea and together we began studying the effects of food insecurity on education and brainstorming ways to create systemic change. They decided to advocate for the creation of a school-based food pantry, a warm and welcoming space accessible to peers. Over the following months, Rebecca and her classmates dialed up local pantries and the handful of school-based pantries across the state. They constructed a cost analysis of what was needed and toured the school scouting for a perfect location. One afternoon Rebecca and a classmate, a young man from Cambodia, asked if they could use my classroom after school. Unbeknownst to me, they had called up the regional food bank and set up a meeting. Hours later, I watched in awe as these two young people, new to the country, sat with representatives from the food bank and confidently proposed a partnership. Within the month, Rebecca, Both, and their class had secured a commitment and a collaboration between the school and the food bank. Mill Market opened down the hallway from my classroom in the fall of 2017. With classmates, teachers, and city officials in attendance, Rebecca and class members, now seniors and wielding oversized scissors from the city's Chamber of Commerce, sliced through red ribbon. As a senior Rebecca became a leader not only in our classroom, but in our school. She was always nearby, always ready to help—walking with a peer to find their class, supporting a classmate who was lonely, translating for a new arrival—endlessly generous with her time. She dreamed of becoming a nurse. Unimaginably, Rebecca passed away in the fall of 2021. Rebecca was a leader, she was an activist, she was a generous, caring young woman and she was an incredible student at our high school. To honor her life, her generosity, and her spirit we dedicated and renamed the Mill Market in her honor. In addition, in the fall of 2021, inspired by and building on the work of Rebecca and her classmates, the city's community foundation partnered with the regional food bank and another nonprofit to replicate the Mill Market our students had championed in other public schools in our city.

—Jessica, teacher and author

In the next chapter we will explore reflection in greater depth through the employment of Reflective Journals and prompts as a way to get students to identify values and begin to apply core ethical principles to real world problems.

Time to Reflect: *How might you manage the logistics of showcasing so students can highlight their work in the best way? How will you facilitate their reflection questions?*

Spotlight on Sources

Generation Citizen: https://kick-start-action-civics.teachable.com/p/foundations1 They have ready-made templates for schools that are just starting with civics projects.

Massachusetts Civic Learning Coalition https://www.macivicsforall.org/ Great resources for anyone connected to action civics projects, not just teachers in Massachusetts.

References

Daniels, D., Merten, M., Manzella, C., Maloney, B., & MacIsaac, D. (2025). Legacy projects: A bridge to sustainable community engagement through civic action pedagogy. *The New England Journal of History*, 82(2), 117–129.

Massachusetts Department of Elementary and Secondary Education (2019). *Civics project guidebook.* https://www.doe.mass.edu/frameworks/hss/civics-guidance.docx

Merriam-Webster, Incorporated. (n.d.). *Merriam-Webster.com dictionary.* Retrieved November 23, 2025, from https://www.merriam-webster.com/

(NCSS). (2013). *The College, Career, and Civic Life (C3) Framework for Social Studies State Standards: Guidance for Enhancing the Rigor of K-12 Civics, Economics, Geography, and History.* https://www.socialstudies.org/standards/c3

6

Ethical Decision-Making

The Key to Shaping Responsible Citizens

Introduction

We all want the people we work with—from politicians and business leaders to our own colleagues—to have strong values and a solid moral compass. In fact, we expect it, even demand it. Yet, these aren't typically subjects taught in school. So, how can we insert values and ethics into our lessons, allowing students to grapple with difficult questions and moral decisions?

This chapter argues that the key is providing students with the time and space to reflect. In our fast-paced, distracted world, taking a moment to reflect allows students to connect with their own values and consider how they would act in a given situation. This practice is the foundation for empathy, helping them understand why others make the choices they do.

This reflection may include really thoroughly examining several things. Students can reflect on what is important to them in different facets of their lives. They can think about things that they have learned over their lives and why they may shape decisions that they make. Potential positive and negative consequences of one's actions and beliefs—with respect to themselves, others, the community and beyond—may either be eye-opening or affirming to their values. Equally important may be the

DOI: 10.4324/9781003746614-6

practice of considering the things that do not align with one's values and determining why.

This type of reflection lends itself to some SEL (social-emotional learning) threads. This may come in the form of engaging in perspective taking, understanding the difference between empathy versus sympathy, discussions of honesty and integrity, and skills for collaboration. The art of disagreeing with civility and listening without thinking of a response are important here as well. There are times in which we think that these "soft skills" are things that all humans innately know; rather, many times these should be explicitly taught in ways that are in context with both the learning objectives and real-life applications.

Some people might think of this as a utopian experiment—having students unplug with journals to explore their feelings about a historical topic. But while maturity comes with age, we all know adults who would benefit from being more reflective and empathetic. What if we, as social studies teachers, could foster that reflection and help it lead to ethical decisions?

Real-World Growth

Picture a male student who, for lack of a better word, is immature. He says things to get a reaction, messes up on purpose, and does his work in a half-hearted way because he can't focus. He struggles with reflection because it's simply not something he's ever done before. Does this sound familiar? Many of us have taught a student just like this.

Now, imagine that same student two years later. As a junior, he is leading a group to create a Land Acknowledgement for the school. He's researching existing acknowledgements, listening to experts, and working with his peers to reach a consensus. He's helping to draft and revise the final document before presenting it to the faculty and the school board. When asked why he decided to join the committee, he replied, "Well, it is the very least any of us could do."

This transformation didn't happen magically. While growing up certainly played a role, the real change came from his opportunity to interact with others, analyze current events, and reflect on what he would do in a given situation. This work allowed him to identify with other groups and their experiences. This chapter will help you build this foundation for your students. While reflection may sometimes feel like busy work, it is often the unseen contemplation that yields the greatest results in the development of character.

> **Time to Reflect:** *What do you do as a teacher to reflect in your day-to-day life, including the successes or challenges of your lessons? How do you model reflective practice for your students or give space for them to reflect both academically and personally? What may be some benefits to this practice?*

The Third Competency: Ethical Decision-Making

The Learner demonstrates integrity, empathy, and responsibility in interactions, balancing competing values, coming to consensus, changing your mind, and compromising.

Associated Skills

To achieve this competency, students will develop the skills outlined in Table 6.1.

Ethics: Moral principles that govern a person's behavior.

Values: A judgment of what is important in a person's life, that guides his or her ethics.

Adaptability: The quality of being able to change when new conditions are introduced.

Accountability: Being held responsible for one's actions.

Priorities: Ranking important things in your life.

Skill EDM1: Value Recognition and Prioritization: *I can identify competing values inherent in complex situations and thoughtfully*

TABLE 6.1 Skills of Ethical Decision

EDM1	**Value recognition and prioritization** I can identify competing values inherent in complex situations and thoughtfully consider how different people or groups might prioritize certain values over others
EDM2	**Ethical principles application** I can identify and apply core ethical principles to analyze real-world problems.
EDM3	**Perspective taking and empathetic reasoning** I can understand the positions of others involved in an ethical dilemma or conflict and consider potential impacts on different individuals and communities.
EDM4	**Collaborate resolution and adaptability** I can engage constructively in discussions to resolve a conflict, look for compromise and commonality, create consensus, and be open to changing my mind when new information emerges.
EDM5	**Responsible action and accountability** I can take responsibility for my decisions and actions and strive to understand the short-term and long-term consequences of others.

Key Vocabulary from Merriam-Webster (n.d.)

consider how different people or groups might prioritize certain values over others.

Reflection, Values, and Ethics

Ethics are the bedrock of society's most esteemed professions—from law and medicine to journalism and education. These aren't just rules to follow, but values that build and maintain public trust. In recent years, a strong push for career readiness has integrated professional skills into high school curricula like criminal justice, business, and STEM. Yet, while we prepare students for these fields, we often fail to introduce them to the very codes of ethics that define those professions until they reach college or even graduate school.

This delay raises a crucial question: How can we equip students with the ethical foundation they need to succeed? This challenge is especially urgent with the rise of Generative AI. As the line blurs between human creation and AI-generated work, students need a strong ethical compass to navigate this new landscape. They must be able to discern what they've created from what was created for them as well as acknowledging the importance of integrity in how they conduct themselves. As educators, we need to instill a core set of ethical principles that empowers our students to analyze real-world problems and make sound judgments.

Before we can get to ethical principles we need to teach students where ethics come from. Values are the decisions on what is important in life, and the values of a person directs the ethical decision that he or she makes. In order for students to understand the values of themselves and others, the best way to accomplish this is through reflection.

> *My class got to talking about ethics and ethical decisions. One of my students sitting closest to the board said he didn't understand what ethics were, and his classmate said, "They're your moral compass." When he still didn't quite understand, his classmate continued, "You know—the things you believe—well those turn into the rules you live by. That's ethics."*
>
> —Anonymous teacher

Reflection is the Vehicle to Values

The Reflective Journal is a great way to highlight the skill **Value Recognition and Prioritization**. It puts students in the driver's seat to think about how they think about themselves, the classroom, the school, and the outside community. Without knowing it, when students reflect, they are tapping into their values to express their thoughts more fully.

> Despite teaching profound lessons that cut right to the hearts of issues, students too easily fall back on the easy rhetoric that their parents and their earlier teachers feed them. They may not fully appreciate the lessons I teach in the moment, but I tell myself that I am planting seeds that they may not see germinate for a decade.
>
> —Anonymous teacher

Every prompt doesn't need to be steeped in meaning, sometimes just starting students off with a prompt asking them to name three things they are grateful for or one thing they are worried about gets them ready to start the class. When looking for meaningful prompts for reflective journaling, however, the best prompts share these qualities:

They are open-ended. A great prompt has multiple possibilities for responses, so that there is no one right answer but a way to have students explore their own thoughts and express themselves authentically.

They are a catalyst for thinking. A good prompt gets students to use their brain. It fosters a connection that a student might not have realized before and moves from passive thought (like memorization) to active thought.

They start the conversation. A good prompt starts with a sentence like, "I used to believe, but" or "One question I still have is______" which gives students the opportunity to take the statement and run with it.

They move beyond recall and foster relevance. By allowing for personal representation you are allowing students to connect their learning of social studies to things that they experience in their lives, anchoring it in their consciousness and promoting connections.

SEL connection: This type of open and individual reflection may put students in the position of considering that they may have changed their position or opinion on things in response to new learning, engaging discourse, or life experiences. Some students may find this uncomfortable, as if they are admitting that they were previously wrong. Having conversations on how sometimes things are not as black-and-white as they may initially seem may be useful in these situations.

Here are some prompts and sentence stems you can try in your classroom:

Prompts About Shifting Perspectives: These prompts are great for reflecting on a change in understanding or opinion.

- I used to think that [person/group] was... but now I realize they were...
- My initial reaction to [event/issue] was... but my current thinking is...
- I used to define [concept] as... but now I would define it as...
- Before this class, my understanding of [topic] was... but now I understand it as...
- I used to see my role in [community/society] as... but now I see it as...
- This challenges what I used to believe about ____________.

Prompts About What You've Learned: These prompts focus on how a specific piece of knowledge or a lesson has changed a student's view of the world.

- A fact or idea that changed my mind was...
- One thing I learned that surprised me was...
- I now question... because...
- Something I've started to think about differently is...
- This discussion has made me reconsider...

- I hadn't thought about __________before, but now I see...
- This connects to what we learned about ____________ because...
- I wonder why__________
- One question I still have is...

Prompts About Empathy and Experience: These prompts encourage students to reflect on how a perspective different from their own has impacted them.

- Seeing the world through [person/group's] eyes made me realize...
- If I were in [person's] shoes, I would have...
- A perspective I did not understand before is... and now I see why...
- This topic has made me more empathetic toward
- I can understand how someone might feel ___________ if they experienced this.
- I now see that [action] can have a different meaning depending on...
- If I put myself in their shoes, I might have _____________

Prompts About Connections and Relevance: These prompts encourage students to connect historical or social topics to current issues, their own lives, or broader themes.

- One thing the topic makes me think about is...
- This event reminds me of...
- Learning about this makes me feel ______ because ________.
- I see how this affected different people in different ways. For example...
- This reminds me of a current issue we see today, such as...
- There is a pattern between __________ and _____________ that I noticed.
- This connects to my own experience because _______________.

- This event influenced the world today by ______________.
- The value this event connects to is ______________.
- It's important to notice whose voice is missing, like ______________.

Where Students Should Write The choice of where students write is flexible and should suit your classroom. You might have them use a dedicated journal you collect and hold onto, a personal composition notebook they bring to class, or even a digital document or survey for a quick reflection. The key is to keep it simple. The less friction there is, the more likely students are to engage.

Making Reflection a Routine Giving students a few moments each day to reflect helps them get better at it. When reflection becomes a consistent part of their routine, it builds a powerful habit. Use the provided prompts to facilitate this process. You can use them as a transition between topics, at the end of a unit, as a bellringer when students first enter the class, or as a preparation for a larger discussion.

Modeling and Sharing To make this process even more effective, model the behavior yourself. Share your own reflections with the class using the same prompts you give to students. Feel free to share when your own perspectives have changed if relevant. This shows them that reflection is a valuable and authentic practice, not just a task for a grade. After students write, encourage them to share their thoughts with a partner or a small group using a Think–Pair–Share activity. This builds a classroom community where communication and different perspectives are valued.

SEL connection: Note that if our students write, we as teachers must read their writing. There are times in which students utilize these opportunities as a way to ask for help and we must be up front with our students (and ourselves) with realistic expectations of how often we read them. Depending on the number of students we have, we may plan to read them once a week or in a rotation that fits our schedule. Giving students the option to "flag" their journal with a sticky note to be read first is helpful and reminding them all that we as educators have the responsibility to share what they write with other professionals should it be necessary is important. Your response doesn't need to be long either; sometimes just a tiny sticker and an underlined sentence or a smiley face is enough to show you read their work. It made you think, and you left something for them.

BEST Practices to Meet Diverse Needs of Learners

- **Bridge** (English/multilingual learners): These students may have schema from other countries to connect to their reflections or may write in the other language(s) that they may know. They may also struggle at first with this type of writing as this may be culturally specific to our schools; co-creating texts in groups with teacher support may be necessary at first to help them engage fully in this style of writing.
- **Expand** (gifted students): Students may engage in research on various local, state, and national politicians' platforms and connect them to various ethics and values. They can also consider local groups, non-profits, and organizations to examine their ideals and connect them to the needs of the community. Students may select certain prompts/topics and document an experience using artificial intelligence to "research" it; they will create a list of different clarifying questions they asked and their evaluation of results.
- **Support** (students with learning challenges or differences): Some students may find the options and the prompts overwhelming; for these students, a smaller selection with some guided discourse before reflecting in writing may be helpful. These students may also benefit from access to graphic organizers or visuals with key facts or phrases based on the prompt/topics they choose.

- **Teamwork**: Students may work in groups to consider the different perspectives of the community and create a guide to better understand them.

Spotlight on Newcomers It is important to recognize that our newcomers come with different schema and experience with respect to government, the roles that citizens may have in the government, and ways that people may use their voices to improve the standard of living. As educators, we cannot assume that our values are universal nor that all students have experiences that support these ideals. This may be an opportunity to connect with newcomers' prior learning and the ways that other governments engage their citizens.

If our newcomers have grade-level literacy (or close) in other languages, this may be a good opportunity to leverage heritage or native languages in creating connections and building schema for them. We can discuss the similarities and differences that they see between what they are learning about the U.S. government and the values and ethics with those of other countries with which they have experience. They may also share their own experiences viewing the United States, both as newcomers and from the perspective of people in other countries.

While we are actively and intentionally creating space for our newcomers to share their points of view and experiences, it is crucial to remember not to judge others' stories or perspectives through our own biases. We may have learned through our lives from certain slants or perceptions about different types of government, different values, or ethics that represent groups that may not align with ours. We as educators must model supportive exchanges of ideas through the lens of learning, kindness, and curiosity.

Examining our Values and the Values of Others

Once students get used to the idea that their perspective shapes the way that they view history and the way that they connect to the world, it might be a good time to bring up the idea of values. Values help give a vocabulary to the priorities that they hold in their life and why they feel that way (Table 6.2). The Social Scientist Brene Brown has done a lot of work with values, and she has identified nearly 150 of them. They include:

TABLE 6.2 Dare to Lead List of Values

Accountability	Equality	Job security	Risk-taking
Achievement	Ethics	Joy	Safety
Adaptability	Excellence	Justice	Security
Adventure	Fairness	Kindness	Self-discipline
Altruism	Faith	Knowledge	Self-expression
Ambition	Family	Leadership	Self-respect
Authenticity	Financial stability	Learning	Serenity
Balance	Forgiveness	Legacy	Service
Beauty	Freedom	Leisure	Simplicity
Being the best	Friendship	Love	Spirituality
Belonging	Fun	Loyalty	Sportsmanship
Career	Future	Making a	Stewardship
Caring	generations	difference	Success
Collaboration	Generosity	Nature	Teamwork
Commitment	Giving back	Openness	Thrift
Community	Grace	Optimism	Time
Compassion	Gratitude	Order	Tradition
Competence	Growth	Parenting	Travel
Confidence	Harmony	Patience	Trust
Connection	Health	Patriotism	Truth
Contentment	Home	Peace	Understanding
Contribution	Honesty	Perseverance	Uniqueness
Cooperation	Hope	Personal	Usefulness
Courage	Humility	fulfillment	Vision
Creativity	Humor	Power	Vulnerability
Curiosity	Inclusion	Pride	Wealth
Dignity	Independence	Recognition	Well-being
Diversity	Initiative	Reliability	Wholeheartedness
Environment	Integrity	Resourcefulness	Wisdom
Efficiency	Intuition	Respect	
		Responsibility	

(Brown, n.d.)

A values list can seem overwhelming at first, but once you begin to explore it, you and your students will find that these values are part of our everyday lives. While this list is not exhaustive, it's an excellent starting point for helping students recognize and prioritize values.

Here are several ways to help your students get comfortable with a values list:

- **Deepen Understanding of Each Value**. Begin by having students explore the definitions. You can give each student the full list and ask them to highlight any words they don't know. Then, have them work in pairs or small groups to discuss their findings before sharing with the class. This is a great opportunity to clarify nuanced meanings. For example, the term "vision" here refers to forward-thinking and planning, not just the ability to see.
- **Collaborate on a Values Glossary**. Assign two or three values to each student and have them create a Google Slide for each one, defining the term and perhaps providing an example. Students can then link their slides together to create a collaborative, online glossary of values that the class can reference throughout the year.
- **Create a Living Values Wall**. Turn a bulletin board into a "Values Wall." Write each value on a sentence strip and post it as a permanent reference. This visual tool helps reinforce the concepts and gives students a resource to consult when they are doing reflective journaling or working through a case study (Figure 6.1).
- **Connect to Personal Beliefs**. Once students have a grasp of the definitions, have them apply the concepts to their own lives. Ask them to identify three values they hold close to their hearts and write about each one in their reflective journal, explaining why these values are important to them. This personal connection will make the abstract concepts concrete and meaningful.
- **Create Class Norms**. Using the values, have students come together to create class norms. Have them pick out no more than five values for the class and then discuss

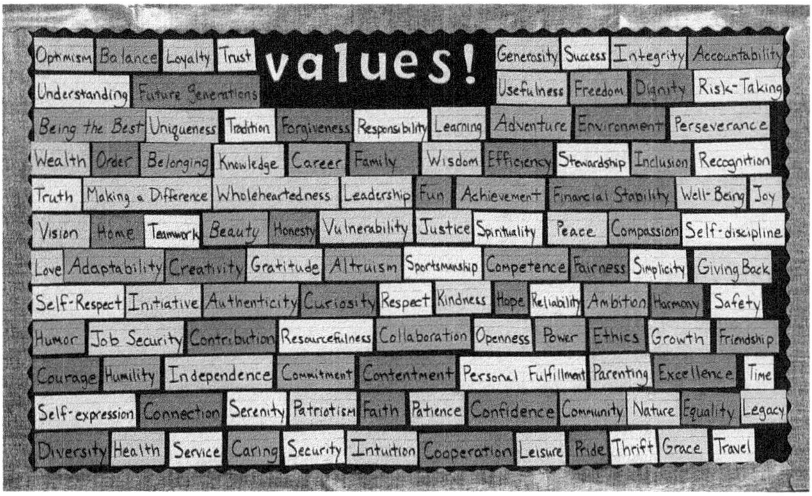

FIGURE 6.1 A list of values as a bulletin board.

what those values look like in practice. Then write them down and have them sign it. It's a good idea to post the norms in the classroom so that you can refer back to them throughout the school year.

- **Reflect Around Languaging**. Compare and contrast different concepts (equality/justice) or discuss if certain words may not adequately translate to other languages while keeping the same meaning (wholeheartedness?).
- **Consider Different Ways to Engage**. Some concepts may look different through the lens of different cultures. Some students may research these values through different perspectives to share and understand them more deeply.

Can't Add Another Thing In? Consider these activities not as replacements for your curriculum, but as ways to create scaffolding. If you have a values glossary or a value wall, you can refer back to it throughout the year. Don't feel like you need to fill up a whole-class period on these activities, maybe you do these for seven minutes at a time. Maybe you plan them during your scheduled half-days when you only see students for a shortened time, or when there's a unit or activity just finishing up but you can't quite start the new topic yet. This work with values are resources you are going to return to again and again. They are worth finding space for in your curriculum.

When Values Collide

Now that students have a solid grasp of what values are, and which ones they hold personally, they are ready to explore how these principles interact—and sometimes conflict—with one another. The following strategies are designed to highlight the skill of Value Recognition and Prioritization in your social studies classroom.

- **Historical Figure Analysis:** After studying a historical figure, ask students to explain their key decisions. Then, challenge them to identify the values that motivated those actions. You can also encourage a personal connection by asking which of those values the student shares with the historical figure.
- **Comparing and Contrasting Values:** When examining a historical debate or conflict, have students analyze the values held by each side. Is the conflict a clash of entirely different values, or are both sides prioritizing the same value but interpreting it differently?
- **Analyzing Social Movement Conflicts:** Use historical movements as case studies in competing values. For example, during the **American Revolution**, the values of liberty and self-determination clashed with the values of order and loyalty to the Crown. Similarly, the Civil Rights Movement pitted the values of justice and equality against tradition and social order.
- **Tracing Shifts in Values:** After studying a person or movement, ask students to explain how a key figure's values appeared to have changed over time. Have them use specific examples to cite that shift. Abraham Lincoln

serves as a perfect example; his initial priority of saving the Union at all costs evolved into a realization that ending slavery was a necessary element to preserve the nation.

- **Through a Lens of Today**: Are there historical figures whose values have been painted in a certain way that may not be accurate to the whole person? How may our modern perspective change the way we think about a person's historical contributions (or not)?

These questions are excellent additions to a student's reflective journal. As the year progresses and students gain a deeper understanding of values, you will be surprised at the growth and nuance in their responses.

> **SEL connection:** Discussions about active listening may be useful when students' values may be at odds with those of their peers. Very often, people listen with the intent to respond rather than truly reflecting on what people are saying—but may not be aware that this is what they are doing. A mini-lesson on ways to listen and learn without response (or perhaps writing the response in one's journal) may be a way to provide a life skill that extends beyond the classroom.

Skill EDM2: Ethical Principles Application: *I can identify and apply core ethical principles to analyze real-world problems*

Values and ethics are intrinsically linked: values are the foundation upon which ethical principles are built. While values are the core beliefs we hold, ethics are the standards and rules that operationalize those values, guiding our day-to-day actions.

However, the connection between a specific ethical standard and its underlying value is not always a straight line. For example, the most famous ethical standard in medicine is "First, Do No Harm." When students are asked to connect this to a value, they might correctly suggest Health, Honesty, Responsibility, or even Service. All of these are excellent answers, demonstrating the complexity of this relationship.

This skill, Ethical Principles Application, is about helping students identify and apply core ethical principles to analyze real-world problems. This ties in seamlessly with current events analysis. Imagine how the classroom conversation around national and world events might shift if students were to view them as ethical dilemmas and conflicts.

Using a Journalist's Code of Ethics

The **Society of Professional Journalists Code of Ethics** (n.d.) provides an excellent framework for this kind of analysis. It is based on four main tenets:

- Seek Truth and Report It
- Minimize Harm
- Act Independently
- Be Accountable and Transparent

Using this code, explore with your students when these principles might come into conflict. For instance, in a breaking news story, a journalist might have to decide what to do when "Seeking Truth" could lead to "Minimizing Harm." This gray area requires the journalist to make a decision based on their own values and an understanding of the ethical framework. This will help foster future discussions about current events too!

A Framework for Ethical Analysis

When applying core ethical principles to either historical or real-world problems, it helps to have a consistent framework for students to follow. Use these steps to guide their analysis every time:

- **Step 1: Identify the Ethical Dilemma**. What is the core conflict? What are the two or more competing values or principles at play?
- **Step 2: Identify Stakeholders**. Who is impacted by this decision, and what is their perspective?

- **Step 3: Apply Ethical Options**. How might a decision-maker weigh the ethical factors? What are the different options they could pursue?
- **Step 4: Justify Your Recommended Action**. After considering the different options, students should make a recommendation and justify it. They must be able to explain why they prioritized one value or principle over another.

Here are some examples of how to bring this skill to life in your classroom:

- **Examine Codes of Ethics:** Have students research different professional organizations and read their codes of ethics. Then, ask them to identify the underlying values they believe are the foundation for those standards.
- **Create Case Studies:** Develop a "What Would You Do?" series of case studies based on historical or contemporary issues. Have students use the ethical framework above to answer the question and provide a recommendation. After their analysis, you can reveal the real-life outcome and have students compare it to their own conclusions.
- **The Words of Others and Ethics:** George Washington wrote out a code of ethics. Theodore Roosevelt spoke about them. Nelson Mandela, Martin Luther King, and Ghandi all shed light on ethics as a call to action. Bringing their words into class during your lessons will always lift classroom conversations.
- **Create a Code of Ethics for Your Classroom:** Different from a "class rules" poster, a code of ethics may build on what they are learning in this chapter to establish a just, safe, and supportive environment for themselves.

Ethics Circles and Bowls

Consider starting an ethics circle in your school and attend the National High School Ethics Bowl! This would give a select number of students the opportunity to dive deeper into ethical questions that affect the world today. Just like there are ethics boards in law, science, and medicine, this gives students the opportunity to talk through thorny problems. This could be a fantastic way to introduce Ethical Decision-Making to the school or deepen the work you've already started. Look for the link at the end of the chapter.

> **Time to Reflect:** *How do you create a safe and non-judgmental classroom environment where students feel comfortable sharing their ethical viewpoints, even if they are unpopular? How do you handle a situation where a student's values or ethical conclusions are in direct conflict with your own?*

Skill EDM3: Perspective Taking and Empathetic Reasoning: *I can understand the positions of others involved in an ethical dilemma or conflict and consider potential impacts on different individuals and communities.*

There are lots of great ways to have students take the perspective of a different person in history or contemporary civics. It's a good idea to have a whole variety of ways that students can understand the positions of others involved in an ethical dilemma. So many students, especially in the early grades of high school, tend to have black-or-white thinking. Helping them to see that people are complex and have complex reasons for making the decisions that they do will help students to foster empathy and even, maybe, a little grace for themselves in the future. This movement into nuanced thinking also helps them to consider potential impacts on different individuals and communities.

Here are ways that you can highlight Perspective Taking and Empathetic Reasoning.

"Stepping in their Shoes" Primary Source Analysis

This activity allows students to develop perspectives by analyzing primary sources through the lens of a specific historical individual or group.

Divide students into groups and provide each with a bundle of primary sources—such as diary entries, letters, newspaper articles, or political cartoons. Assign a historical figure or group to each team and have them determine how that person would react to the sources. Together, they will decide what their assigned persona would do, feel, or respond. After sharing their reactions with the whole class, have them write a letter or journal entry from that person's perspective to solidify their view and its resulting actions.

A great journal prompt might be: ***"Seeing the world through [person/group's] eyes made me realize..."***

SEL connection: Many students may not have well-developed vocabulary in terms of emotions or perspectives. These activities may be a good opportunity to engage them in describing ways that the historical figure may have felt in various parts of their experiences and also ways that they perceive the students themselves may have felt in similar situations. They also may liken some of the recollections shared in the primary sources to things that may occur today.

Mock Trials or Debates

Stage a historical debate or mock trial where students take on specific roles and positions. The Ratification Debates, the Scopes Trial, the Sacco and Vanzetti trial, or *Korematsu v. United States* are all excellent options.

The key is to give students solid sources and talking points. As the "judge" for the case, ensure each side gets equal time. Consider having each student craft their own opening argument to see the unique thinking behind each approach. Conclude the activity with a debriefing session where each side must articulate and compliment a strength of the opposing team's argument or delivery.

A great journal prompt at the end of this lesson might be: ***"One challenge of the perspective I represented was ____________ because..."***

Throw me a RAFT

The **RAFT** writing strategy is a powerful tool for social studies, allowing students to step into the shoes of historical figures. This long-standing method encourages students to think critically about the purpose and audience of their writing, making the assignment more engaging and authentic. Developed by Nancy Falck and Christy Young (1987), RAFT is an acronym, which stands for Role, Audience, Format and Topic. Let's examine each component:

Role: This is the perspective the writer takes on. Instead of writing as themselves, the writer takes on a new identity, such as a specific historical figure or more generalized character.

Audience: This specifies who the writing is going to. It influences the tone, language, and details for the piece of writing.

Format: This is the kind of writing. Will the student be writing a letter? A speech? A diary entry? A newspaper?

Topic: The subject the student is writing about. This is always tied to the curriculum and is often the capstone to the learning unit.

A great example here might be after studying industrialization to have students create a RAFT from the perspective of a Lowell Mills Girl. Here is what it might look like:

Role: A young woman that works at the Lowell Mills

Audience: The young woman's family

Format: A letter

Topic: Life working in a mill, the daily schedule, the positive and negative aspects of the job and living with other young women.

LEA (Language Experience Approach)

Using the Language Experience Approach (LEA) is a way to engage students in considering their senses when writing a story. While this type of activity is usually about an event or time that the students themselves have experienced (class trip, assembly), this strategy may be adjusted to write from the point of view of a historical figure or to better explain a time in history. If we consider the young woman in the Mill from our RAFT activity, this is a great start to an LEA writing.

This type of engagement is particularly powerful for many reasons. Students will consider the way things may have sounded, looked, smelled, or felt when considering this story—when typically they may not think about this type of detail. Students (particularly multilingual learners) may have the opportunity to write about a historical event in the present tense using sentence starters and frames, which may engage them in language that is more familiar and easier to manage (Salva & Matis, 2025). Gifted students may focus most on dialogue and can even research some of the more common uses of language of the time period in the story that may not be in use today.

Many times, LEA may be a strategy that teachers use while co-creating a text together as a group or a class. When the teacher is the scribe, this may be a way that supports the whole class in the writing process, learning vocabulary, and sentence structure. The teacher models the thought process and the organization of the story/recollection. Co-creating texts may also be something students do in either heterogeneous or homogeneous groups—depending on the task and goals. Important to note is that any of these literacy approaches or techniques may be great starting points for our civics classes, but going "rogue" and adjusting the assignments or rules for the strategy may make it even more engaging for all students.

Time to Reflect: *At times, it may be difficult for students to go beyond their own viewpoints. What can you do to help them see beyond their own perspective to better empathize with others' experiences and feelings? How do you help students understand the difference between sympathy and empathy and how may this improve understanding of diverse perspectives?*

Skill EDM4: Collaborate Resolution and Adaptability: *I can engage constructively in discussions to resolve a conflict, look for compromise and commonality, create consensus, and be open to changing my mind when new information emerges.*

Coming to consensus is so uncool in today's "gotcha" world, and yet it can be deeply satisfying not only to reach consensus, but to feel (as a student) that you have been seen and heard by your classmates. Teaching students the difference between dialogue, discussion, and debate will help them to foster civic dialogue, become better listeners, and gain the skills necessary for civic engagement

In their book, *Becoming Active Citizens: Practices to Engage Students in Civic Education Across the Curriculum* (2022), authors Tom Driscoll and Shawn McCusker created a great table for the difference between discussions, debates, and dialogues (Table 6.3).

> One important thing I hammer home is that debating should be a healthy way to explore new ways of thinking. We must acknowledge that we have differing opinions about almost everything. I model respectful discussion techniques, like asking clarifying questions and I stress that my opinions are my own and they can think differently than I. Sometimes, we will do a silly "debate" about the best pet, season or sport. This allows students in a less intense situation to see a respectful conversation with differing opinions.
>
> —Dan, history teacher

Yes, And

Encourage students to build upon each other's answers by modelling the concept of "Yes, And" where when one person makes a suggestion, or gives an answer, another student who wants to add will start it with, "Yes, and…" This may be used as a way to build schema on a topic and work collaboratively to engage with peers in either a formal or informal way.

TABLE 6.3 Differences Between Discussions, Debates, and Dialogues

Discussion	*Debate*	*Dialogue*
Offers thoughts and ideas	Achieves or wins	Broadens personal perspective
Seeks answers and solutions	Seeks weaknesses	Seeks shared meaning
Persuades others	Emphasizes disagreements	Identifies area of agreement
Shares information	Focuses on right or wrong	Uncovers areas of ambivalence
Avoids conflict and differences	Emphasizes conflict and differences	Articulates conflict and differences
Maintains relationships	Ignores relationships	Builds relationships

(Driscoll and McCusker, 2022)

Suggest concrete and creative activities for teaching this subtopic. For each activity, include a brief description of how to implement it in the classroom. There are several ways to provide access to this type of activity. A video of students comically doing this activity can demonstrate the idea and students can even use visuals or signs to share the steps they are taking or modeling. Providing graphic organizers and time to prepare for students who may use that time to work through languaging and content can be beneficial to meaningful participation.

I foster civil discourse by drawing parallels between past events and modern-day issues. History gives us the advantage of distance—we can examine what happened without the immediate polarization of current debates. Using that as a vehicle, I encourage students to move beyond surface facts (what an artifact shows or what a letter says) and think critically about the social, political, economic, religious, and governmental contexts behind them. By identifying patterns, considering where things went wrong, and exploring how societies attempted to address challenges, students practice respectful dialogue about complex issues. This approach helps them recognize nuance, listen to different perspectives, and use history as a guide for engaging with diverse opinions in the present.

—Kaitlyn, adjunct history professor

Building Consensus Through Dialogue

This lesson, modeled on the "Talking about Local Current and Contested Issues in Schools" (TALCCS) by Street Law, Inc. (n.d.), provides a structured way to help students engage with polarizing topics, build arguments, and practice seeing an issue from multiple perspectives. The core of this activity is to help students feel **seen, heard, and respected** while grappling with complex issues.

The TALCCS Method

First, choose a polarizing issue, like the use of the atomic bomb. Prepare a worksheet with ten arguments for the issue and ten arguments against, with one set on the front and the other on the back. It's helpful to number them.

Next, divide students into groups of four (or six, but an even number is best). In each group, assign two students to argue "for" the issue and two to argue "against."

Initial Argument Selection: Give students time to read through all the arguments. Then, each side—the "for" team and the "against" team—should choose and write down their top three arguments. When both sides are ready, they'll present their positions to the other side.

Switching Perspectives: Now comes the twist. The teams switch sides. Each team must then choose two of the best arguments the opposing team just made. They can't just pick their own arguments from the original list; they must select from what was presented to them.

Building a New Case: After selecting the two arguments, each team revisits the original worksheet to find a new, third argument to add to their case. The teams then come together again to present their revised positions. This time, they should acknowledge and compliment the other side for the two arguments they kept before presenting their full three-point case.

Reflection and Consensus: Once the presentations are done, each student should share their personal thoughts on the topic and reflect on whether their view changed because of the exercise. While the goal is not necessarily to reach a consensus, the process itself is invaluable. It teaches students how to build on the ideas of others and truly understand the opposing viewpoint, even if they don't agree with it.

> **Time to Reflect:** *So often we reward students for winning a debate. How can we reward them for coming to consensus, building upon each other's answers, or reaching a compromise? How do we demonstrate value in working together towards a common goal when we do not always agree on every aspect of an issue?*

Skill EDM5: Responsible Action and Accountability: *I can take responsibility for my decisions and actions and strive to understand the short-term and long-term consequences of others.*

Perhaps one of the most profound quotes from Norton Juster's *The Phantom Tollbooth* is this quote:

> You must never feel badly about making mistakes…as long as you take the trouble to learn from them. For you often learn more by being wrong for the right reasons than you do by being right for the wrong reasons.
>
> (Juster, 1961/2011, p. 258)

The truth is that helping students take responsibility for their decisions and actions is not one teacher's responsibility, or one department's responsibility alone. It is necessary to have a whole-school model, with administrators who uphold the rules, and help the teacher in administering the rules. Many schools are moving toward the restorative justice model, where students are asked how they can take accountability and make amends in order to create a more inclusive and understanding school community, and this chapter lends itself to that model of school discipline.

> *Like all teachers in my school, I have to take a few of the after-school detention duties. What I choose to do is have my students write what they did wrong, and what they can do to either make the situation better, or what they can do to avoid the situation the next time. They aren't excused until they turn that piece of paper in. I then send it to the teacher that assigned the student detention, to see that the student had given their actions some thought.*
>
> —Anonymous teacher

There are lessons through this chapter that will help your students see that there are values associated with decisions. Through their reflective journals, they will come to understand themselves and others better. Through the exploration of values, they will be able to tie decisions to those values, both of themselves and of others.

Artificial Intelligence and Free Choice

When introducing the use of AI in the classroom, it's essential to address academic integrity head-on. Rather than simply banning AI, you can engage students in a discussion about their personal values or help them develop class norms. This collaborative process empowers them to understand why using AI to complete assignments for them goes against the shared ethical code of the classroom.

Ultimately, the goal is for students to actively choose to be responsible for their own work. By connecting the use of AI to a discussion of ethics and shared values, you can create an environment where students understand that academic honesty isn't just a rule, it's a reflection of their commitment to learning and their respect for the community.

This is a good segway to discuss the word integrity and the value we place on one's own voice and hard work. AI can be a tool that helps us in different ways (much like when Google first became part of our world) and establishing guidelines for use as a community is crucial. If your school or district doesn't have an academic policy on use of AI, please start these conversations with your administration about the responsible use, ways to cite it, and the specific situations in which it may be permissible. The sooner everyone is on the same page, the better it will be for all involved.

Time to Reflect: *What can you do to facilitate a class community that relies on values and class norms to allow students to make the right decisions? When they falter, how can you facilitate ways for them to take responsibility for their decisions and actions? How can we make this part of the norms to reflect on our interactions and words along with the ways that they affect our communities?*

Spotlight On Sources

Street Law TALCCS https://streetlaw.org/who-we-are/about/

Saint Anselm Ethics Circles https://www.anselm.edu/about/offices-centers-institutes/centers-institutes/center-ethics-society/programs/student-programs/programs-high-school-students A good way to learn how high schools are addressing ethics and an introduction to ethics circles and ethics bowls.

Brene Brown Dare to Lead https://brenebrown.com/hubs/dare-to-lead/ Connected to her book, this has information about using the values chart.

National High School Ethics Bowl: https://nhseb.org/ This would be a fantastic way to have your students, and your school, address ethics head-on.

References

Brown, B. (n.d.). *Dare to lead list of values*. Brené Brown. Retrieved November 23, 2025, from https://brenebrown.com/resources/dare-to-lead-list-of-values

Driscoll, T., & McCusker, S. (2022). *Becoming active citizens: Practices to engage students in civic education across the curriculum*. Solution Tree Press.

Falck, N. R., & Young, C. L. (1987). RAFT: A writing strategy that works. *Reading Improvement*, 24(3), 200–204.

Juster, N. (2011). *The phantom tollbooth* (J. Feiffer, Illus.). Knopf Books for Young Readers. (Original work published 1961)

Merriam-Webster, Incorporated (n.d.). *Merriam-Webster.com dictionary*. Retrieved November 23, 2025, from https://www.merriam-webster.com/

Salva, C., & Matis, A. (2025). *Boosting achievement: Reaching students with limited or interrupted formal education*. Seidlitz.

Society of Professional Journalists. (n.d.). *SPJ code of ethics*. Retrieved November 23, 2025, from http://spj.org/spj-code-of-ethics/

Street Law, Inc. (n.d.). *Talking about local current and contested issues in schools (TALCCS)*. Retrieved November 23, 2025, from https://www.streetlaw.org/

7

Critical Thinking

The New Frontier of Literacy

Introduction

What if the most important lessons a student needs to learn in your classroom has nothing to do with the causes of the Civil War or the details of the New Deal? What if the most valuable skill you impart is the ability to look at a claim, question its source, and see the hidden agenda behind it? The role of the social studies teacher is changing. We are no longer just historians; we are navigators helping students chart a course through a sea of information, disinformation, and deepfakes. This is about teaching them to be their own best thinkers, armed with the skills to analyze, question and ultimately understand the world for themselves.

> **Time to Reflect:** *What's your biggest worry when it comes to teaching about disinformation? What are potential results or consequences in teaching it?*

DOI: 10.4324/9781003746614-7

The Fourth Competency: Critical Thinking

Critical Thinking: The learner analyzes information, identifies bias, forms reasoned opinions, identifies conflicts of interest, and identifies uses of propaganda.

Associated Skills

To achieve this competency, students will develop the skills outlined in 7.1.

TABLE 7.1 Skills of Critical Thinking

CT1	**Information Analysis and Evaluation** I can effectively break down complex information from various sources (textual, visual, digital, AI), identifying key arguments, evidence, and possible influencing factors.
CT2	**Bias and Perspective Recognition** I can identify different types of bias within information, distinguish between fact and opinion, and recognize perspective and context.
CT3	**Reasoned Opinion Formation** I can synthesize and analyze information and evidence and create a well-supported opinion while acknowledging counter arguments.
CT4	**Conflict of Interest Identification** I can recognize and explain various conflicts of interest and how these conflicts can influence decisions and actions.
CT5	**Propaganda and Manipulation Detection** I can identify common propaganda techniques in the media and explain how these techniques are designed to persuade or manipulate audiences.

Key Vocabulary from Merriam-Webster (n.d.)

Bias: prejudice in favor of or against one thing, person, or group compared with another, usually in a way considered to be unfair.

Propaganda: communication that is designed to influence an audience to advance an agenda, often by using biased, misleading, or emotionally-charged messages.

Manipulate: control or influence (a person or situation) cleverly, unfairly, or unscrupulously.

Skeptical: not easily convinced, having doubts or reservations.

Persuade: cause (someone) to believe something, especially after a sustained effort; to convince.

Disinformation: false information that is intended to mislead.

Artificial Intelligence (AI): computer systems that create in a way that used to rely on human thinking but now can be generated via computer.

Skill CT1: *Information Analysis and Evaluation I can effectively break down complex information from various sources (textual, visual, digital, AI), identifying key arguments, evidence, and possible influencing factors.*

In a world overflowing with data, the ability to discern and evaluate information is more critical than ever. It's easy to assume we're immune to deception, but with disinformation being a strategic tool for individuals, corporations, and even nations, we need to be prepared. As social studies teachers, our role is to equip students with the skills necessary to navigate this complex landscape.

It's not just about consuming information; it's about actively deconstructing it. This involves identifying core arguments, scrutinizing evidence, and recognizing the underlying influences that shape the message. This skill is essential to critical thinking, empowering students to move beyond passive acceptance and become informed, discerning individuals. Whether making sound financial decisions, understanding a political debate, or evaluating a viral social media post, mastering this skill is essential for success in all aspects of life.

Textual Analysis: Starting with Primary Sources

For history teachers, the most logical starting point for building this skill is through the analysis of primary sources. Before diving into the document's content, it's essential to provide students with the necessary context. Pose key questions to guide their thinking, possibly in the Six W format:

- **Who** wrote the document?
- **What** was its purpose?
- **When** was it written?
- **Where** was it written?
- **Why** was it written? (or Who was its audience?)
- **How** was it received?

Step-by-Step Document Deconstruction

A structured approach to primary source analysis ensures students gain a deep understanding. A great example to illustrate this is Abraham Lincoln's The Gettysburg Address.

Analyze the Vocabulary: Begin by having students scan the document for unfamiliar words or phrases. This step, while it may seem painstaking, is crucial for comprehension. For example, what does "four score and seven years ago" actually mean? By breaking down the vocabulary—like explaining that a "score" is twenty—you can help students connect the address back to a significant historical event. Subtracting 87 years from 1863 brings us back to 1776, the year of the Declaration of Independence. This simple act connects the text to a broader historical narrative.

Read for Understanding: Once vocabulary is clear, have students read the document for content, pausing occasionally to check for comprehension. Encourage them to summarize sections in their own words.

Rewriting for Comprehension: Finally, have students rewrite the document in their own words. This exercise forces them to process the information and demonstrate a true understanding of the text's arguments and meaning. For The Gettysburg Address, this can help them see how Lincoln's words connect back to the principles of 1776 and articulate what he meant by a "new birth of freedom."

But what happens when there are differing accounts of an event? How can students make sense of an event from two different perspectives? This requires careful curation on your part to make sure that students are reading about the same event from different points of view, and able to differentiate the key arguments, give evidence, and identify possible influencing factors.

SEL connection: Students may write a flowchart of differing perspectives and what may be the reasoning behind these points of view. They can then make a connection to a controversial issue that is relevant today. It is important for them to realize that we may disagree with viewpoints of others but it is important to understand the reasons why they feel that way; this provides context and allows us to see the full picture.

There are some great sources out there, though, if you are short on time. The Digital Inquiry Group, originally distributed through Stanford University, but now its own nonprofit, has curated groups of primary sources in both the world history and American history spheres. Likewise, Gilder Lehrman Institute of American History has over 300 primary sources that teachers can use in their classroom. What's nice about these sources is that they have been created by historians who are asking the right questions and curating the documents to help students arrive at the answers. Students will still be challenged, but you can spend your time creating scaffolding or working on your BEST practices for diverse learners. Both sources are at the end of this chapter.

BEST Practices to Meet Diverse Needs of Learners

- **Bridge** (English/multilingual learners (MLs)): For MLs with literacy in other languages, translations of the clarified passages for students with learning challenges may give access to these documents. It is important to recognize that clarification of these documents must be done before translating to increase the likelihood that the translation is a valid one (without outdated or incorrect word equivalents). For MLs without literacy in other languages, summarized versions of these documents or information written in outline form in phrases may be ways to engage them in the overarching ideas of the times and movements.

- **Expand** (gifted students): Students can create a visual about the varying perspectives of the time (Enslaved peoples, Northerners, Southerners, Indigenous peoples, Free People of Color, People in other countries) and determine where some perspectives overlap and others may be at odds with each other.
- **Support** (students with learning challenges or differences): As these documents are dense with challenging or dated vocabulary, the word analysis may be more in depth with clarifying glossaries or word banks available. Students may also benefit from a clarified version of the document alongside the original written in a lower lexile level as relevant to literacy needs.
- **Teamwork:** Students can work in groups to design a children's book translated into other languages about Lincoln or another leader of this time period that may give insight into this time period.

Spotlight on Student Leaders: This is tough material that might be more challenging for some than others. Consider implementing a Critical Thinking Peer Mentorship Program. This initiative shifts student leaders from delivering presentations to providing personalized support. Leaders can be thoughtfully paired with students needing help with research, social media anxiety, or essay structure. The mentor's role is to use skills like Conflict of Interest Identification to help the mentee decode social media bias or use Reasoned Opinion Formation to build a strong counterargument for a tough paper. This model empowers student leaders as Information Resilience Trainers and provides tangible, one-on-one skill development for their classmates.

Visual Literacy: Analyzing Images, Videos, and Charts

Students are constantly consuming a flood of visual information from social media, news, and digital platforms. It's crucial for them to develop the ability to analyze and evaluate what they see, rather than just passively absorb it. By encouraging students to be skeptical, you equip them with a powerful tool to question the immediate claims of an image and actively seek evidence to back them up.

A Structured Approach to Visuals

One of the most effective ways to foster visual analysis is to create a guided, inquiry-based experience. Instead of telling students what a piece of art or an image means, provide them with a framework to discover its meaning on their own. This approach encourages a deeper, more meaningful engagement with the material (Figure 7.1).

The painting *American Progress* by John Gast, 1872, is an excellent example for introducing the concept of Manifest Destiny.

FIGURE 7.1 American Progress by John Gast. (Gast 1872).

To begin the discussion, simply ask your students two key questions:

- "What is happening in this painting?"
- "What is the evidence?"

Wait patiently as students make their own observations. They will point out a half-clothed spiritual figure floating over the landscape, the division between light and dark sections of the land, and the different animals and modes of transportation depicted. The power of this exercise lies in the collaborative process—building on each other's answers, navigating awkward silences, and allowing them to arrive at the conclusion themselves.

Once the class has identified and discussed the various elements, you can bring it all together by asking, "Based on everything we've observed, what is the artist's argument about Manifest Destiny?"

This type of exercise reinforces the analytical questions, "What is happening?" and "What is the evidence?" By consistently applying this process, students will naturally become more skeptical and discerning when they encounter visual information in the future.

Political Cartoons

Political cartoons are often harder for students to ascertain the central meaning of, and yet it is important for them to wrestle with the discomfort of not quite knowing what it all means. Addressing this head-on sometimes helps by saying, "It's OK if you feel uncomfortable with this, or if this is hard; we are going to push through this discomfort to get stronger at this skill." Here is a good example from Michael Angelo Woolf (1837–1899) gotten from the Digital Commonwealth Massachusetts Collection Online (Figure 7.2).

You can certainly use the same exercise as the painting exercise above, and it will give you very good results. However, you can also try the Political Cartoon Analysis from the National Archives (n.d.), which helps students look at the cartoon with an eye toward analysis:

FIGURE 7.2 Political cartoon example. (Woolf, 1861).

Analyze a Cartoon

Meet the Cartoon

Quickly scan the cartoon. What do you notice first?

What is the title or caption?

Observe its Parts

WORDS:

Are there labels, descriptions, thoughts, or dialogue?

VISUALS:

List the people, objects, and places in the cartoon.

List the actions or activities.

Try to make sense of it

WORDS:

Which words or phrases are the most significant?

List adjectives that describe the emotions portrayed.

VISUALS:

Which of the visuals are symbols?
What do they stand for?
Who drew this cartoon?
When is it from?
What was happening at the time in history it was created?

What is the message? List evidence from the cartoon or your knowledge about the cartoonist that led you to your conclusion.

Use it as Historical Evidence

What did you find out from this cartoon that you might not learn anywhere else?

What other documents or historical evidence are you going to use to help you understand this event or topic?

Time to Reflect: *How may we consider historical events differently through a lens of today's values? Does that change the perspectives of the events? Do the messages resonate today?*

Digital Information

Our students are saturated in information on the internet, and they often struggle to distinguish between valid information and disinformation. We frequently overlook a critical fact: being a "digital native" does *not* automatically equip students with the skills to responsibly navigate the constant inundation of data—it's like trying to drink from a fire hose.

> One of the main challenges I've experienced in teaching critical thinking through civics and social studies is competing with student attention spans—sometimes it feels like my lectures are up against the latest TikTok trend or video game. To address this, I started incorporating short TikToks into my lessons. This helps deliver

basic information in a format students connect with, freeing up class time for deeper conversations. From there, I focus on discussion—asking for their opinions, posing guiding questions, and encouraging them to draw their own conclusions or parallels.

—Kaitlyn Mulrane, Adjunct History Professor

The severity of this gap was highlighted by Stanford University's 2016 study on Civic Online Reasoning. Researchers found that students "lacked basic skills of digital evaluation," leading the study to conclude, "The results—if they can be summarized in a word—are troubling" (Breakstone et al., 2019). Specifically, students demonstrated an inability to discern which websites were accurate, to identify the sponsors of a study, or to detect potential bias in sponsored content.

This challenge is not limited to youth. Adults are only half as likely to choose a true news story over a false one, and many struggle to determine the reputability of information sourced from popular platforms like TikTok, YouTube, or even established websites (Angelucci & Prat, 2024).

To address this critical deficit, Stanford researchers determined what skills students needed to become responsible consumers of online media). Their solution focuses on teaching Lateral Reading as a superior alternative to traditional Vertical Reading. Vertical Reading reads from top to bottom of a website's content, trying to determine what is written is true without looking at bias, sourcing, or funding, oftentimes because those factors are not available for immediate consideration. Lateral Reading shifts the focus from deep analysis of a single source to quickly evaluating the source's credibility by looking at *what other reliable sources say about it*. Instead of asking, "Is this article true?" the consumer asks, "Is this source trustworthy?" (Wineburg et al., 2016)

When we encounter information online, how can we effectively discern if what we are seeing is real, true, and accurate? Lateral Reading provides a powerful, proven framework.

Teaching Lateral Reading: SIFT

Mike Caulfield of the University of Washington and Sam Wineburg of Stanford University have worked hard to come up with ways to verify online information in a fast and easy way. In their book *Verified: How to Think Straight, Get Duped Less, and Make Better Decisions about What to Believe Online* (University of Chicago Press, 2023), they were smart and created the acronym **SIFT**. It stands for: **Stop, Investigate, Find, and Trace**. Let's go into a little more detail:

STOP. Pause and reflect before passing this on or using it as a source. Is it designed to create an emotional reaction?

INVESTIGATE the source. This is done by Lateral Reading, going out of that website, opening up another tab, and investigating what other sources say about that tab.

FIND better coverage. Look for other, more reliable sources that report on the same claim and make comparisons to the original website.

TRACE claims and quotes back to the original context. What is the original source using as its justification and can you back those claims and quotes up with digging?

With this information, we can create an easy notecatcher for students to make determinations about sources (Table 7.2).

TABLE 7.2 SIFT Components

SIFT Component	*Questions to Consider*	*Lateral Reading Technique*
Stop	How is this source making me feel?	Paying attention
Investigate	Who is behind this site or who is paying for it?	Google the source with the words "bias" or "funding"
Find	Is this claim common knowledge or an isolated incident?	Search the core claim with a trusted news source that follows a journalistic code of ethics
Trace	Is this claim/fact/quote presented accurately or is it out of context?	Look at the embedded links. For pictures, use a reverse image source (like Google Lens or TinEye)

Website: Describe what you see
Is this course credible? Yes/No
Explain your reasoning with text evidence.

Valid or Vile? Online civic reasoning can't just be a "one and done" lesson. Like a muscle, it needs to be exercised over and over again in order for it to be strong. This can feel overwhelming and exhausting. Consider having a weekly website for students to explore called "Valid or Vile" or some other catchy term that you can think of. Students are given a website that they need to use the SIFT analysis on, and determine Valid or Vile and give reasons why. You could also invite students to suggest websites or go through the analysis together on it. This could be a good bellringer activity or something you do every Friday morning, etc.

Crash Course to Help Lighten the Load

Luckily, the makers of Crash Course have teamed up with Mediawise and Poynter.org and together they designed a series connected to Navigating Digital Information, which you can use in conjunction with your lesson. These videos would also be a great way to introduce the information you are about to teach. It's a 10-part series that encourages students to become "more active consumers of information." Quite honestly, we could all use as much help as we can get on this topic!

Artificial Intelligence and Detecting Deepfakes

We have been made to believe that "seeing is believing," but like the old saying goes, "Don't believe everything you see and only half of what you read." AI is literally getting better every single day, and detecting deepfakes will become increasingly harder.

Perhaps we should stop right here and define a deepfake. According to Merriam Webster (n.d.), a deepfake (noun) *is an image or recording that has been convincingly altered and manipulated to misrepresent someone as doing or saying something that was not actually done or said*. They are intentionally made to have the viewer get the wrong impression, idea, or opinion. This is a good time to remind students to be skeptical and that the SIFT analysis may be able to be employed here as well.

The Three Ds

Teaching a stand-alone lesson here, separate from Lateral Reading, would still be a good idea, as more information is being created by AI and there are more deepfakes that are being employed. At this point even some of our elected officials are posting deepfakes on their social media pages without a disclaimer that they are deepfakes, or maybe even just meant to be humorous.

A good way to approach teaching about deepfakes is the Three Ds: Define, Detect, and Debate.

Start with Define. Begin by asking the students to define what a deepfake is, and then asking them to find one that they know for sure is a deepfake. Give them a minute or two to find an example. Then if you are comfortable, ask them to show the deepfake to the people at their table. Ask students if they notice any commonalities amongst the deepfakes and then put the commonalities on the board.

Move to Detect. Next you can ask students to help to detect what are "tells" of a deepfake, including extra limbs or fingers, fuzziness around a part of a picture, different paces of movement in the video. Scientists at Northwestern University have published a 50-page paper on ways you can determine if something was created by AI or is a deepfake; the link is at the end of the chapter. This could be helpful for students to see subtle ways in which a picture can be manipulated or created from scratch.

On to Debate. Have students debate the ethical consequences of AI-generated deepfakes. Sure sometimes they can be fun, but how could they hurt someone? Be sure to talk about people who might be hurt in an active way (for example, by ruining their reputation), but also how someone might be hurt in a passive way (a model not getting a job because they used an AI picture instead). Have students decide how to make the use of AI-generated pictures and deepfakes more equitable, or have students create a set of rules to be followed when it comes to generating deepfakes.

Try this powerful extension. If you are instituting a regular "Valid or Vile" analysis for websites, maybe mix the assignment up once in a while with a deepfake detector.

A Note on Artificial Intelligence in Class

There are benefits and challenges with the use of AI with students and in the school setting. Many educators would like to ban usage based on dishonesty, or other ways that they feel students will engage AI to do their work for them. By this point, all educational settings should have a policy (or one in the works) on the use of technology and AI for students. We would like to share some insight into ways that we can provide guidance for ethical usage.

As noted in this section, students may have opportunities for critical analysis of information in terms of determining the authenticity of resources and how to check and counter reference sources. They may also learn more about refining questions and identifying key terms that will help them cultivate a search for information that guides them most succinctly.

As much as we may want to block our students from using technology in this way, we need to reflect on AI usage and the district policy (a) must be current and (b) must respect the changing platform of technology. We don't want students simply using AI instead of writing their own work; however, these tools may be useful in brainstorming or in giving additional direction or viewpoints. Rather than restricting all use of AI, guidance on how to use it ethically and in certain circumstances may be more beneficial for our students in the long run.

Time to Reflect: *It's really easy to feel overwhelmed when it comes to teaching about misinformation. What are some ways that you can share your concerns about misinformation with your students that are both helpful and constructive? Are there ever times in which misinformation is helpful?*

Skill CT2: *Bias and Perspective Recognition I can identify different types of bias within information, distinguish between fact and opinion, and recognize perspective and context.*

Understanding Bias

We are all biased in some ways, which is simply a tendency or inclination toward one thing, person, or group over another. Sometimes these inclinations are harmless, such as always parking in the same spot in a parking lot or having a favorite burner on the kitchen stove. However, bias is often discussed in a way that is considered unfair or prejudicial.

The challenge for students is recognizing when they encounter bias, and learning to discern the perspective, context, and intent behind it. This is especially true in the media. Pieces of media—like advertisements trying to get a reader to choose one kind of deodorant over another, or campaign ads promoting one candidate—are intentionally created to promote bias in the reader.

Explicit Versus Implicit Bias

When examining bias, it's vital to differentiate between its two forms: explicit and implicit.

- **Explicit Bias** is a preference you are aware of and can readily articulate. For example, you may have an explicit bias toward ordering Italian food at a restaurant because the flavors are familiar and similar to the food you grew up with. You know you prefer it and why.
- **Implicit Bias**, on the other hand, is a preference that operates outside of your conscious awareness. Keeping with the food example, you might be unconsciously avoiding the new sushi restaurant because you have an implicit, unexamined bias that makes you associate unfamiliar cuisines with risk or a bad experience, preventing you from even trying to find a dish that suits your palate.

> **SEL connection:** While explicit bias is viewed as something intentional and implicit is something that may even be unconscious, they are both harmful. Students can reflect on situations shared about both historical and current events, thinking about the perspective that they most relate to and consider why. Are there preconceived notions that they may have about certain groups or political views? Are there subsequent events that shaped our notion of what or who is "right" and "wrong" in this situation?

Recognizing External Influence

Many external factors can influence or create these biases. Consider the pressure to choose a specific restaurant:

The bias in the information around you such as a billboard showing an enticing plate of chicken parmesan, a friend's recent enthusiastic talk about lasagna, or a coupon for a particular eatery is designed to entice you. These outside influences are manipulating your choice, but because the source of the influence is obvious (an ad, a coupon), if you pause to reflect on your decision, you can likely recognize the intent behind the bias. The goal is to get students to identify bias, discern between fact and opinion, and recognize perspective and context, all in an environment that is designed to distract.

Avoiding Bias (as Much as Possible!)

Sometimes when it comes to teaching students, we want them to avoid bias in order to make the stream of information more reliable. With this being stated, we acknowledge that we all have bias and the reflection through this lens may allow us to seek information that is as unbiased—or at least as open about potential bias—as possible. When we look at an example from teaching current events from Chapter 4, how do you help students locate a source that is less biased, in order to get as close to the news as it actually happened, rather than a hyped-up version of what happened? Sometimes, we let other people do the work for us.

Organizations like All Sides Media have studied 2400 different news sources, done surveys on the languaging, and taken averages to arrive at their media bias chart. You can find this chart at https://www.allsides.com/media-bias/media-bias-chart.

One way to address media bias is to have students only look at news stories from the middle three columns, keeping the far columns out of play. This only solves a short-term problem, however. It does not help students to identify media bias; it just eliminates it. It's a good first step, perhaps, but not the answer to the problem all together. At the same time, it's nice to know that this kind of chart is out there, and if you don't see a source that your students are interested in using for their current event, they have an app that gives information on over 2400 sources.

Identifying Loaded Words and Tone

Words are not neutral. The use of them can totally change the way you envision an event happening. These can be put into four different categories: Supportive, Neutral, Negative, and Highly Negative. Let's say that the president, while walking across a room, trips over the edge of the carpet. Here's what the media might say:

Supportive: President recovers quickly after brief stumble on carpet.

Neutral: President trips on carpet while crossing room.

Negative: President nearly falls amid health concerns about balance.

Highly Negative: President goes flying after tripping on carpet, causing a national scene.

For the lesson, consider creating a chart with the four different categories. Have three different clips of news events ready and then ask students to write a sentence describing the event from each of the four different bias categories.

Euphemisms and Dysphemisms

A *euphemism* is when you make something sound better than it actually is, and a *dysphemism* is the opposite—you make something sound worse than it actually is. Like the activity above, you can give students examples of statements and have them re-write them euphemistically and then dysphemistically. Here's an example:

Neutral Statement: The company fired 50 employees due to a reduction in its quarterly budget.

Euphemism: The company streamlined its operations by releasing 50 team members.

Dysphemism: Fifty hardworking people axed in the company's greedy quest to make more money.

Another way you can accomplish this is to use the All Sides Media Bias Chart and have students find three titles from three news sources (Far Right, Center, and Far Left) on the same topic and then have them compare the wording of the titles.

This exercise tips into when neutral fact turns into opinion, especially if adjectives are employed, such as *hardworking* and *greedy*. This is a very powerful way for students to examine the way that they are digesting news and the way the words are being employed to shift their perceptions. Reflection will be very rewarding for them here. At the end of the lesson, consider asking students to reflect on how the use of words can change the perception of events.

Context and Perspective

Context is the background information, circumstances, or conditions that surround and clarify an event. Adding context helps determine the intent and provides a factual basis for understanding the event. Perspective is the subjective point of view from which a person perceives or understands an event. It is colored by their values, experiences, and relationship to the event. Giving students a neutral event and then showing how the context and perspective shape the neutral event.

Neutral Event: A teacher sent an email to a parent at 11:30 p.m.

Context: The Why and the When: A teacher sent an email to a parent at 11:30 p.m. because the grade portal was down for maintenance.

Parent Perspective (Negative): The teacher sent an email much too late and needs to have better boundaries around my family's time and privacy.

Parent Perspective (Positive): This teacher is incredibly dedicated to make sure I know about my child's grade before school the next morning.

Jumping to Conclusions

The example above can lead to a great mini-lesson on the idea of jumping to conclusions. Both the negative and positive parent perspectives are based upon their own personal assumptions connected to the neutral event, and are connected to emotional reactions. Pointing this out to students will allow them to avoid the danger of an emotional reaction and seek out the context of the situation.

> **Time to reflect:** *What examples will you use for the teaching of bias, the power of words, context and perspective, and jumping to conclusions? Do you have any examples from your own life that resonate with these lessons? How can you engage students in this type of reflection without discounting their views and lived experiences?*

Skill CT3: *Reasoned Opinion Formation I can synthesize and analyze information and evidence and create a well-supported opinion while acknowledging counter-arguments.*

The Five-Paragraph Essay

There are lots of ways to teach this skill, but when it comes to social studies, perhaps the best skill we can impart on our students is the ability to execute the five-paragraph essay. Though many schools have turned away from the five-paragraph essay, surprisingly colleges are turning back to the old-fashioned blue book and essay response. Why? Because in the age of generative AI, the five-paragraph essay, written in person, continues to be one of the best indicators that a student can understand the material and create a brief, reasoned argument.

Distinguishing Social Studies from Language Arts

Crucially, the five-paragraph model serves a different purpose in social studies than it does in Language Arts (LA).

While students learn structure in LA by analyzing a single primary text (literature) for meaning and effect, the social studies essay demands a higher standard of proof. A historical essay requires the synthesis of multiple external sources such as facts, data, and competing historical interpretations to argue for causation and impact.

To help students manage this increased complexity, moving from single-source interpretation to multi-source synthesis, we can utilize an easy graphic organizer. This framework is designed to help students organize their thoughts, integrate evidence, and ensure they meet the specific requirements of a historical argument, regardless of their prior experience with essay writing (Table 7.3).

Essays Evaluating Two Arguments

Likewise, helping students to be able to evaluate two arguments, or competing arguments helps them to reason out their opinion while acknowledging the other side's valid arguments. The graphic organizer has slightly different requirements of a historical argument, regardless of their prior experience with essay writing (Table 7.4).

These may seem easy, but that's only because we naturally know how to do this as educators, and as people who have gone through the system. These graphic organizers can help students to organize their thoughts so that they can get down to the

TABLE 7.3 Historical essay five paragraph graphic organizer

Title:
Paragraph One: Hook, background information, Thesis Statement
Paragraph Two: Topic Sentence, Supporting Argument A
Source:
Paragraph Three: Topic Sentence, Supporting Argument B
Source:
Paragraph Four: Topic Sentence, Supporting Argument C
Source:
Paragraph Five: Restating Thesis in a new way, Summarize Supporting Arguments, Concluding Thought

process of writing and making their arguments both clear and concise. Don't underestimate the power of a good graphic organizer to help students clear the clutter from their thoughts and get down to business.

BEST Practices to Meet Diverse Needs of Learners

- **Bridge** (English/multilingual learners): Ensuring that the students understand the purpose of the traditional five-paragraph essay with the different components is essential. Exemplars and graphic organizers in the format of an outline will be key for showing this type of writing for those who may never have done it before. As different cultures have different styles and standards for writing, this type of support is helpful for both organization and for the purpose of the task.

TABLE 7.4 Five Paragraph Graphic Organizer Comparing Two Arguments

Title:
Paragraph One: Hook, background information on two arguments, Thesis Statement choosing a side.
Paragraph Two: Topic Sentence, Supporting Argument A
Source:
Paragraph Three: Topic Sentence, Supporting Argument B
Source:
Paragraph Four: Debating the positive and negative aspects of Arguments A and B.
Paragraph Five: Restating Thesis in a new way, Summarize Supporting Arguments, Concluding Thought

- **Expand** (gifted students): Students will add specific theory and research with citations into their essays, along with those of the opposing viewpoints. An extension to this may be analyzing these sources through the lens of bias and determining the purpose and slant of the author/speaker.
- **Support** (students with learning challenges or differences): Giving students access to the various perspectives and viewpoints represented in these writing tasks through different modalities may give them a more well-rounded understanding of the assignment. They may also benefit from a graphic organizer that is specific to the social studies essay format, particularly with the additional standards of proof needed.
- **Teamwork:** Students can work in groups to write scripts to imagine the background of various historical

arguments/documents. The different perspectives can be presented in ways that demonstrate that there are often many "right" answers based on what people perceive to be best for themselves and the nation at the time.

Skill CT4: *Conflict of Interest Identification. I can recognize and explain various conflicts of interest and how these conflicts can influence decisions and actions.*

This skill mirrors the skill EDM3: Perspective Taking and Empathetic Reasoning. The difference is that in Perspective Taking and Empathetic Reasoning, we are trying to understand the *feelings, beliefs, or values* behind a decision. However, in Conflict of Interest identification, we are trying to understand what are the *motivations, incentives or financial stakes* behind a decision. While the first skill allows students to be empathetic to decisions, the second skill encourages students to be skeptical of a decision. (Skepticism seems to be a common theme of this chapter!)

Time to Reflect: *How do we encourage students to be skeptical without encouraging them to be jaded instead? How do we model this behavior? What is the appropriate role of optimism here?*

There are three conflicts of interest that students should be able to see in their own lives. Giving an example of different conflicts of interest that students might understand from their kitchen table, scout meeting, school board, or local legislators might help them to understand how conflicts of interest are a part of our everyday lives. Connecting this to Ethical Decision-Making from the previous chapter will help them to see that every day there are decisions to be made, that are rooted in values, with respect to matters connected to conflicts of interest. It's not easy, but here are some examples:

Financial When a person or organization stands to gain or lose money based on a decision or statement. *A pharmaceutical company CEO argues that their new, expensive drug should be mandatory for a common condition.*

Personal/Political When a person's reputation, political standing, or family relationship could influence their judgment. *A town council member votes to award a major construction contract to their sister-in-law's company.*

Professional/ Duty When a person has a primary duty to one party, but takes an action that benefits a secondary party. *A doctor who is paid by a specific medical device company recommends* only *that company's product to all their patients.*

Here are some lessons you can try with your students:

- **Who gets the contract?** Present students with a fictional, simple decision (e.g., "A school must select a vendor for new uniforms"). Provide profiles of three committee members, each with a different hidden conflict of interest (COI) (one owns stock in a textile company, one's child is the star athlete who wants a specific brand, and one is retiring soon and wants the process to be over quickly). Students identify the COI and predict how each person will vote, explaining *why* the incentive trumps objectivity. Then have them identify a best case scenario (a fourth person, perhaps) who should get the contract.
- **Hidden Conflicts of Interest**. Have students look at celebrity endorsements and expert testimonies. Why might a celebrity or athlete endorse a certain product? Consider looking at college student athletes and their ability to have endorsement deals. Why might they choose to endorse a product that they might not use? Likewise, when it comes to "expert" testimonies, how can we tell if a person is really an "expert" not a paid actor? Using a version of the SIFT analysis might help here.
- **Mission v. Money**. Come up with an ethical dilemma that students need to work through. For example, "A major university needs a large donation. A fossil fuel company offers to build a new science wing but demands the university shut down its climate change research center." Divide students into different groups (University President, the Head of Climate Research, the Student Body, the Donor, the community or town, etc). Each

group must identify their group's *own* conflict of interest and then present their solution to the problem of funding, acknowledging how their stake makes them biased.

> **SEL connection:** Conflict resolution (both in person and on digital platforms) is something that many students find challenging. This may be an opportunity to discuss respectful discourse when one fundamentally disagrees with someone. There are times in which there should be this discourse and there are others in which each can share their thoughts and they respectfully agree to disagree.

Skill CT5: *Propaganda and Manipulation Detection. I can identify common propaganda techniques in the media and explain how these techniques are designed to persuade or manipulate audiences.*

All the Feels

At the heart of propaganda is emotion. Maybe it's glittering generalities to inspire hope, patriotism, or pride. Maybe the propaganda is designed to promote fear, or fear of missing out. The good news is that propaganda has been around for centuries. The bad news is that propaganda has been around for centuries. So you won't have to worry about running out of examples!

Like a great magician, a piece of propaganda is designed to control an audience's focus through misdirection, control perception, and, of course, never give away their tricks!

The trap, ultimately, is that students don't believe that they are as foolish or gullible as people of the past, that they would *never* fall for that silly propaganda. Everyone thinks that they are wiser than that. We as educators have to show that we are just as susceptible today as we were at the founding of the nation. Leaning into the term skeptical will help with this lesson, again.

In this lesson, you can find examples from any time period, to show pride, hope, fear, patriotism, responsibility/duty or fear of missing out. Like skill CT1, you can ask students "What is happening in this poster?" and "What is the evidence?" Then review the definition of propaganda. Propaganda is the deliberate, systematic dissemination of information (facts, arguments, rumors, half-truths, or outright lies) with the single purpose of manipulating public opinion, beliefs, or actions to benefit the sponsor's specific agenda, usually connected to the public's emotions.

Once you show the piece of propaganda, ask students if it fits the definition of propaganda, and then ask them what manipulation is taking place, and what the emotion it is connected to. Then ask them to compare pieces of propaganda from history to today. Here is an example (Figure 7.4).

Example: Propaganda Posters of Pride

Have students compare a propaganda poster of pride from World War II and the present day. The World War II poster (Figure 7.3) and a recent poster from Immigration and Customs Enforcement (n.d.). The posters can be placed side by side on a screen so students can note various similarities or differences. Encourage students to compare the two posters for similar themes and messaging. Ask them if they believe the poster from 2025 is meant to look like the World War II poster on purpose (Figure 7.3).

This can be done over and over again. Having students see that messaging is similar will help them to see that people can be enticed repeatedly to the same themes.

The Essential Mission: Teaching Truth in the Digital Age

Teaching critical thinking is perhaps the most important thing we can do as teachers, and yet it's a never-ending battle, especially with the information bombardment that our students face every single day.

Fighting against disinformation, propaganda, and manipulation is not a sidebar activity; it is the new frontier of literacy. If we don't equip students with the ability to question information and assess its source, we fail in our most basic duty to prepare them for civic life.

FIGURE 7.3 Works Projects Administration (WPA) Poster from World War II. WPA Poster, 1942 (Ritter, 1941).

Teaching Students to Build their Own Boats

Think of the information overload as a flood, and our students as simply swimming to survive. Our job isn't to dam the flood; it's to teach them how to build their own boats. We must encourage students to transition from being passive consumers of content to active navigators of information. This means:

- **We Teach the Tricks, Not Just the Facts:** Just as a magician relies on the audience not knowing the secret, a propagandist relies on the audience not knowing the technique. When we teach students to identify the loaded words, the

FIGURE 7.4 Ice and Customs Enforcement (ICE) poster. Immigration and Customs Enforcement (n.d.).

conflict of interest, and the propaganda techniques being used, we are permanently exposing the trick.

- **We Prioritize the Source Over the Story:** We must shift the focus from *what* is being said to who is saying it, why, and what context is missing. This is the core skill that allows students to navigate any information landscape, regardless of the topic.
- **We Validate Their Struggle:** It's hard work to be a thoughtful citizen. Remind students that pausing to check a source or analyze a bias is an act of intellectual courage—a vital contribution to the future of their communities and our democracy.

Your persistent effort in the classroom is what builds resilient, informed citizens who can think for themselves. That's not just a teaching goal; that's a necessity for the future.

> I try to use history as a vehicle to teach critical thinking—it is not the dates and battles that are important to me but rather the lessons on how to be a critical thinker that I try to use with my students. It is important to influence thinkers rather than give the class what I want them to believe. That is why for many things in a history class it is important to give both sides of the story and have the kids make the decisions from there.
>
> —Matt, history teacher

The late Jane Goodall (2002, p. 11) leaves us a quote that sums this up, "You cannot get through a single day without having an impact on the world around you. What you do makes a difference, and you have to decide what kind of difference you want to make."

Spotlight on Sources

Digital Inquiry Group: (https://www.inquirygroup.org/history-lessons)

Gilder Lehrman Institute of American History (https://www.gilderlehrman.org/)

Crash Course Series on Navigating Digital Information: https://thecrashcourse.com/topic/navigatingdigitalinfo/

Northwestern University Paper on Deepfakes: https://arxiv.org/abs/2406.08651.

Common Sense Education has a specific lesson plan titled "Are Deepfake Videos a Threat to Democracy?" that includes a video, slides, and a "Manipulated Media" analysis handout. https://www.commonsense.org/education/digital-citizenship/lesson/are-deepfake-videos-a-threat-to-democracy

PBS NewsHour Classroom offers the "AI Unlocked" series, including a lesson on "Recognizing AI-generated content" with objectives, a warm-up, and discussion questions. https://www.pbs.org/newshour/classroom/lesson-plans/2025/04/recognizing-ai-generated-content

MIT's Media Literacy in the Age of Deepfakes is a deep-dive module with a syllabus, bibliography, and an exploration of synthetic media for civic good (e.g., an art installation about a fake failed moon landing). https://deepfakes.virtuality.mit.edu/

PBS NewsHour/MediaWise has lessons on teaching Media Literacy including deepfakes. https://mass.pbslearningmedia.org/collection/be-mediawise-news-literacy-lesson-plans/

References

Angelucci, C., & Prat, A. (2024). Is journalistic truth dead? Measuring how informed voters are about political news. *American Economic Review*, 114(4), 887–925. https://doi.org/10.1257/aer.20211003

Breakstone, J., Smith, M., Wineburg, S., Rapaport, A., Carle, J., Garland, M., & Saavedra, A. (2019). *Students' civic online reasoning: A national portrait*. Stanford History Education Group & Gibson Consulting, 1. https://purl.stanford.edu/gf151tb4868

Caulfield, M., & Wineburg, S. (2023). *Verified: How to think straight, get duped less, and make better decisions about what to believe online*. University of Chicago Press.

Gast, J. (1872). *American progress* [Painting]. Autry Museum of the American West.

Goodall, J. (2002). *The ten trusts: What we must do to care for the animals we love*. Harper One.

Merriam-Webster, Incorporated. (n.d.). *Merriam-Webster.com dictionary*. Retrieved November 23, 2025, from https://www.merriam-webster.com/

National Archives. (n.d.). *Analyze a cartoon* (Intermediate) [Worksheet]. National Archives and Records Administration. Retrieved November 23, 2025, from https://www.archives.gov/education/lessons/worksheets/analyze-a-cartoon-intermediate

Ritter, W. (Photographer). (ca. 1941). *Become a nurse your country needs you* [Poster]. ANMM Collection, Australian National Maritime Museum.

U.S. Immigration and Customs Enforcement. (n.d.). *Return to mission* [Digital poster]. U.S. Department of Homeland Security. November 23, 2025, from https://www.ice.gov/return

Wineburg, S., McGrew, S., Breakstone, J., & Ortega, T. (2016). *Evaluating information: The cornerstone of civic online reasoning* [Technical Report]. Stanford History Education Group. http://purl.stanford.edu/fv751yt5934

Woolf, M. A. (1861). *Our national bird as it appeared when handed to James Buchanan, March 4, 1857. The identical bird as it appeared A. D. 1861* [Lithograph]. Digital Commonwealth, Boston Public Library. https://www.digitalcommonwealth.org/search/commonwealth:9880w8854

8

National and Global Awareness

The Whole Enchilada

Introduction: The Call for Global Citizenship

We live in a global community. With 195 countries, 193 of them active in the United Nations, the United States is just one piece of a vast, interconnected whole. All nations constantly interact to manage global catastrophes like pandemics, climate change, world wars, and economic meltdowns. Countless decisions are made daily around the globe that profoundly affect our students' lives and learning.

But how aware are our students? Teacher anecdotes suggest low engagement, with one confiding she felt she'd have to set herself on fire to capture their attention. However, this perception masks a powerful reality: some of our students are wise beyond their years. They come from vastly different experiences and hold a wealth of knowledge about global customs and cultures. Treat their personal histories as classroom resources! While students are more connected than ever via social media, they may only be seeing a curated, narrow window of the world based on their likes and clicks, missing the larger picture of global interconnectedness.

Our mission to teach good citizenship must evolve. It can no longer be limited to self-reflection or a national focus. It must

DOI: 10.4324/9781003746614-8

expand to include a deep understanding of the world and its interconnectedness. All students (and humans) must understand that citizenship starts in their own backyards. Understanding local government and their own roles in it does not sound like a first step—but it is crucial in finding their voice. This extends to understanding national and world events and perspectives. Their everyday decisions—what they eat, what they wear, how they travel—all have a global impact. After all, as the famous Disney song goes, "It's a small world after all."

You may find that your students have varied perspectives and experiences with respect to global engagement. This is where differentiation and your own reflection come into play. We can't assume that all students have the same lived experiences or points of view regarding global events or even types of societies around the world. This chapter will help with strategies to teach the different organizations that work in concert to try to reach world health, peace and security—no small feat!

Time for Reflection: *How comfortable are you teaching about the interconnectedness of the world? Are there any parts that you need to brush up on so that you can answer students' questions fully? Are there potential implicit biases to consider when speaking about other countries or areas of the world?*

The Fifth Competency: National and Global Awareness

National and Global Awareness: The learner can recognize the interconnectedness of global issues and effectively problem-solve using systems thinking and an understanding of cause-and-effect relationships, treaties, and international bodies.

Associated Skills

To achieve this competency, students will learn the skills outlined in Table 8.1.

TABLE 8.1 Skills of National and Global Awareness

NGA1	**Global Systems Analysis** I can identify and describe the roles and functions of major international organizations and key international agreements, explaining their significance in addressing global challenges.
NGA2	**Interconnectedness Recognition** I can explain how local, national, and global issues are interconnected, and how events or policies in one area can have a ripple effect on other areas.
NGA3	**Cause and Effect in Complex Systems** I can analyze complex national and global problems by identifying multiple causes, predict short- and long-term effects, and recognize feedback loops within these systems.
NGA4	**Multi-Level Governance Understanding** I can differentiate between the different jurisdictions and responsibilities of local, state, and national governments, and explain how these governments interact with each other and with international bodies to address national and global issues.
NGA5	**Global Problem-Solving Approaches** I can propose and evaluate different approaches to addressing national and global challenges, considering diverse perspectives, ethical implications, and the effectiveness of certain strategies.

Key Vocabulary from Merriam-Webster (n.d.)

Interconnectedness: *the state of being connected with each other.*

Multilateral: *agreed upon or participated in by three or more parties, especially the governments of different countries.*

Feedback Loop: *a process where the outputs of a system are circled back and used as inputs.*

Jurisdiction: *the official power to make legal decisions and judgments.*

Governance: *the action or manner of governing.*

Skill NGA1: Global Systems Analysis: *I can identify and describe the roles and functions of major international organizations and key international agreements, explaining their significance in addressing global challenges.*

It's a part of the developing teenage mind to not think too closely about chain reactions or cause-and-effect scenarios. Oftentimes as the adults in their lives, we need to walk them through those steps. *If I use the money now to buy food through Doordash, I won't have enough money later to buy the concert tickets that I really want* is a hard concept for them because they are hungry right now. Likewise, leading our students through the complex realities of interconnected global relations is a challenge because students don't necessarily need to know the information right now, but they do need to know it someday.

The key is to get students to be able to make the connection between their everyday experiences and the world around them, to look at the behind-the-scenes work that happens every day to get their food on the table, shoes on their feet, or smartphones in their hands. Getting students to pay attention long enough to truly reflect on concepts that are not visible to them is often a challenge.

> I've always heard the adage that "all history is local," but until I started looking at the world through micro-history, I never really understood it. It only takes understanding that Connecticut's thriving wood trade literally fueled sugarcane furnaces while its staves were the container for the related molasses and rum trade, to see how interconnected the world is.
>
> —Rhonan, history teacher

The United Nations

The first stop in teaching interconnectedness in the world is the United Nations. The United Nations was born as a result of World War II, in 1945, when 50 nations came together in San Francisco. Its core mission was to be a permanent forum where nations could resolve disputes through diplomacy rather than warfare, guaranteeing fundamental human rights and establishing the basis for international law.

Over the years, the UN's responsibility has grown and shifted. It has three primary responsibilities. The first responsibility is Maintaining International Peace and Security, helping to prevent conflicts or provide humanitarian aid to areas in conflict. The second responsibility is Protecting Human Rights. The third responsibility is Fostering Development, or eradicating hunger, poverty, and disease, and increasing education, around the world.

The first step to teaching the United Nations is to teach the reason for the United Nations: World War II. Ideally, this would happen in a class that has just learned about World War I, the failure of the League of Nations, and World War II, but if you needed to, you could give a brief lecture (5–10 minutes) to get the students up to speed. Have students begin with this quote from Franklin Roosevelt, and have them re-write it in their own words:

> In our disillusionment after the last war we gave up the hope of achieving a better peace because we had not the courage to fulfill our responsibilities in an admittedly imperfect world. We must not let that happen again, or we shall follow the same tragic road again—the road to a third world war.
>
> January 6, 1945 broadcast by FDR

Then have students read the UN Charter Preamble:

We the Peoples of the United Nations Determined

to save succeeding generations from the scourge of war, which twice in our lifetime has brought untold sorrow to mankind, and to reaffirm faith in fundamental human rights, in the dignity and worth of the human person, in the equal rights of men and women and of nations large and small, and to establish conditions under which justice and respect for the obligations arising from treaties and other sources of international law can be maintained, and to promote social progress and better standards of life in larger freedom,

And for These Ends

to practice tolerance and live together in peace with one another as good neighbours, and to unite our strength to maintain international peace and security, and to ensure, by the acceptance of principles and the institution of methods, that armed force shall not be used, save in the common interest, and to employ international machinery for the promotion of the economic and social advancement of all peoples,

Have Resolved to Combine Our Efforts to Accomplish These Aims

Accordingly, our respective Governments, through representatives assembled in the city of San Francisco, who have exhibited their full powers found to be in good and due form, have agreed to the present Charter of the United Nations and do hereby establish an international organization to be known as the United Nations.

After reading the preamble, have students determine the problem that needs to be solved, and the mandate of the new organization. Consider having the students write out which phrase they like the best or that speaks to them the most, and share it with the class, along with why they chose it. As a possible extension, you could have students compare it to the Preamble of the US Constitution for commonalities and differences.

After students understand the scope and charge of the United Nations, it is a good time to discuss exactly *how* all of those goals will be achieved. This will segway you nicely into the organizations within the United Nations. There are a lot of them, so this might take more than one lesson.

Essentially, there are five main organs of the United Nations, and then dozens of sub-organizations. They are located all over the world.

The five main organs are a good way to start. Assign or have students form five groups (one for each organ). Each group will quickly research and create a "snapshot" of their assigned organ with responsibilities and location (four of the five are in New York City; the International Court of Justice is in The Hague, Netherlands) The organs are:

General Assembly: The deliberative, policymaking, and representative organ. They make recommendations and decide the budget. Each country gets one vote, but can have up to six representatives.

Security Council: Primary responsibility for international peace and security. They impose sanctions, authorize military action, and create peacekeeping missions.

Economic and Social Council: Coordinate economic and social work of the UN. They promote higher standards of living, human rights, and global health

Secretariat: Carry out the day-to-day activities of the UN.

International Court of Justice: Legal arm of the UN. They settle disputes between nations.

(There is a sixth organ called the Trusteeship Council, that is now inactive).

After students have researched their organ, have the groups create a single slide for the class that they can present, with appropriate pictures added to the information on the slide.

Then once students understand the basic systems of the United Nations, they can choose their own organization that they are interested in studying more and being able to tell the class about. Consider thoughtful pairing of students or allowing students to work alone if they want to, in order to create information for their peers about the different organizations of the UN.

Here are the main Operational Arms of the United Nations. They are responsible for executing the UN's mandates on the ground, ranging from human rights protection and disaster relief to financial stability and setting global standards. The United Nations has a great graphic that explains which organ oversees which organization: https://www.un.org/sites/un2.un.org/files/un_system_chart.pdf

Once students are able to report out to their peers about what each organization does, you will be able to layer on some other organizations while keeping the knowledge of the United Nations intact. The key is the base of the United Nations for students, and then layering on the extra organization will help them to conceptualize the complex nature of regulation for the world. It's important to remember that all of the organizations above represent the United Nations.

SEL connection: As students are looking through the various organizations, they can consider concrete ways that specific ones may support target groups, i.e. children, homeless people, immigrants, or others. In their opinion, what would be ways that these organizations can demonstrate "success" (or what evidence can they find that these organizations are making a difference)?

Model UN Simulation

If your school doesn't have a Model UN club, consider starting one. In Model UN, students learn about complex contemporary issues, are assigned roles as nations and in different international organizations, and are given a certain scenario that they need to become experts on. Students need to research how their country feels about the scenario, and are able to write a paper from the position of that nation. They then travel to a central location and take on the role of diplomacy in real time. They debate, craft alliances, and create solutions. They work hard on compromises and have fun doing it. Prizes are given for best delegate, best negotiator, and best paper to name a few. Sometimes, there is a silly scenario that breaks the tension of the real-world problems—think of invasion from aliens or the creation of an overly large pizza that nations are fighting over. It's the skills of problem-solving, negotiation, coming to compromise, and presentation that they are able to hone during this set of simulations. There's a link at the end of the chapter to get you started.

Skill NGA2: *Interconnectedness Recognition. I can explain how local, national, and global issues are interconnected, and how events or policies in one area can have a ripple effect on other areas.*

Global Supply Chain Challenge and the Ripple Effect

Choose a familiar item with a complex origin (like an avocado, coffee beans, chocolate, or dragonfruit (think dragonfruit refreshers!). Then divide students into four teams: Origin, Global Production, National Market, and Local Consumption. Each team needs to research and trace where their object comes from, possible issues that might impact the production and cost, and how it travels to the next destination. Let's use the example of chocolate chips:

Chocolate Chips

Origin: (Côte d'Ivoire, Ghana or Ecuador) Students research where chocolate comes from, how it is grown, what it does to the environment, who provides the labor, and any concerns they might have. How are the raw materials shipped?

Global Production: (The Netherlands, Belgium, Switzerland, or Malaysia) Students need to find the importers and how they produce the beans into parts that are re-exported across the globe, like cocoa liquor, butter, and powder. How is it packaged and shipped around the world?

National Market: (United States) Hershey, Nestlé, or Mars, taking the parts of cocoa products and creating chocolate chips for national consumption. Companies also use other ingredients: Where do they come from? How are they packaged and shipped around the country?

Local Consumption: Chips bought by a bakery, using other ingredients: Where do they come from, and where are they sold locally? How are they packaged for a local audience?

After students research and report out, devise some scenarios as to problems that might occur with the supply chain. Some examples might include

- Choosing a cocoa bean grower that does not use child labor.
- A drought that affects the crops.
- A shortage of oil for transportation.
- A strike of factory workers due to low wages.
- A high tariff on cocoa impacts national imports.

Have students guess whether each of these things would lower or raise the prices and have them attempt to explain why they think that is. Finally, have students create a flowchart and/or map as to the progression of the chocolate chips, so that they can see how many people work for them to have their chocolate chip cookie, considered the most American of cookies, because they were invented in the United States (in Whitman, Massachusetts). Ask them, "What is the ripple effect" on their item and what are the results?

Here are some other lesson plan ideas to help your students learn about interconnectedness:

- **Deconstruct your favorite meal**. Have students choose a favorite meal, get an ingredient list and then trace the location of manufacturing or growing for each item, then have them report on it to their class with a map to show the locations of the different ingredients.
- **Where do your sneakers come from?** Have students look at the sneakers, say how much they paid for them, then find out who manufactured them, where the factories are, and who works there. If it's possible, have them find out what the hourly wage is for the workers (or what the average worker gets paid in that industry and area).
- **Smartphones**. Similarly, have students research the essential minerals that are needed for smartphones, where they are mined, how they are transported to factories and then how they are manufactured and shipped to the United States. This would be a good lesson for reusing and recycling as well, to see if there was a way to reuse those minerals since they are in limited supply, and are environmentally damaging to mine.
- **Carbon Tax Debate**. Present a real or hypothetical Local Policy (e.g., a city council votes to ban plastic bags) or a National Policy (e.g., a government passes a significant carbon tax). Then, in a jigsaw activity, assign students roles to research the Local, National and Global implications.

BEST Practices to Meet Diverse Needs of Learners

- **Bridge** (English/multilingual learners): Word banks will be very helpful here for your multilingual learners (MLs), as well as sentence stems. These are words that students might not have had much exposure to at all. Also, considering the cultural aspects of "interconnectedness" may be necessary to engage MLs as both learners and teachers; they may be able to share their own perspectives of connections from other cultures or share if they have knowledge or experiences from other countries. Consider using different maps than the standard one that puts the United States in the center of the map. It allows students to think of the interconnectedness of the world from another vantage point.
- **Expand** (gifted students): It's possible that gifted students can research their own topic and report out on ripple effects without breaking into groups. Students can also meet with local representatives to learn about their stances and perspectives on tariffs through the lens of how the United States interacts with other countries.
- **Support** (students with learning challenges or differences): Visuals, and perhaps a video that takes students through the different parts of these problems, may provide context before students go through these activities. Maps here will definitely help as well as a flowchart from the beginning of the supply chain to the end of the supply chain.
- **Teamwork:** Students may work in pairs or small groups to research these various topics through a common thread: How do these products impact our lives currently and potentially lives in other settings (rural, urban, suburban)? What is the effect on the environment of these products? What is the effect of artificial intelligence on the environment and civics as it is currently available?

The above examples are all contemporary examples, but systems thinking is important throughout history as well. Think of the Triangular Trade (otherwise known as the Transatlantic Slave Trade) or the Cotton Economy as examples.

> **Time for Reflection:** *If you only had time to teach one of these concepts, which would you choose? Why do you think this concept is either most important or more accessible to students?*

Skill NGA3: *Cause-And-Effect in Complex Systems. I can analyze complex national and global problems by identifying multiple causes, predict short- and long-term effects, and recognize feedback loops within these systems.*

Governance and Economic Security

It's really hard to keep all of the organizations straight that the United States belongs to, how we interact with the other participatory countries and what each organization does—or does not do—in the world. Sometimes, it just seems like a whole bunch of acronyms or alphabet soup. It's important to teach about the UN before you teach this lesson, so that students know the basics about the enormity of the structures. The organizations below set the rules for the global economy, trade, and financial systems. They will help teach about complex cause and effect problems using a simulation style of lesson (Table 8.2).

Global Crisis Response Simulation

We live in a world where a collapsing economy, a major war, or a devastating natural disaster can quickly spill over national borders, overwhelming the resources of any single country. When these massive, complex crises hit—whether it's a crippling debt

TABLE 8.2 International Organizations

Organization	*Acronym*	*Primary Role and Global Significance*
United Nations	UN	The chief organization for diplomacy, peacekeeping, human rights, and development; serves as the central forum for addressing almost all global challenges.
International Monetary Fund	IMF	Works to secure global financial stability by providing loans and structural adjustment programs to countries facing economic crises.
World Bank	IBRD/IDA	Aims to reduce poverty by offering loans, credit, and grants to governments for development projects (infrastructure, health, education).
World Trade Organization	WTO	Regulates international trade by negotiating trade agreements and providing a framework for members to resolve trade disputes.
G7/G20	G7/G20	Forums for the world's most advanced and emerging economies to coordinate on macroeconomic and financial policies to ensure global growth.

crisis, a regional conflict, or post-disaster recovery—, no one government can handle it alone. This lesson will give students the background they need to begin navigating this interconnected world.

Step One: Research and Report. Have five posters up around the room with the title of each of the organizations listed at the top of each poster. Divide your class into five groups, where each group will become "experts" for one of the international organizations. On the poster, they should list at least three of their organization's specific powers, responsibilities, and tools. After 15 minutes, groups report about their organizations.

Note for collaborative groups: Groupings for collaborative learning may be effectively designed in different ways with various outcomes. Students may choose their groups; this may increase their interest level and potentially decrease their on-task behavior (depending on the group!). While this is certainly favored by students, the composition of the group may not fit all tasks. There may not be a student with strong reading comprehension or someone who is organized and those may be skills necessary for the success of the group in certain activities. Heterogeneous intentionally designed groups may allow teachers to establish a group that has a variety of strengths for best results. Homogeneous intentional grouping may group together students with similar interests, reading levels, languages, or other strengths with the specific task in mind. Teachers who do this may differentiate the task or topic to best meet the strengths of the groups. Whatever method one uses to set up collaborations in class, it is important to mix them up often so all students have the opportunity to connect with as many peers as possible over the course of the year or semester.

Step Two: Crisis Scenarios (Short- and Long-Term Effects). After the groups report out, read the different crisis scenarios below. For each scenario, groups must decide: Who would be the lead organization, what is the short-term action, what is the long-term consequence, and who must work in concert?

- A country's currency is collapsing, and it can't pay its short-term debts.
- Two nations are fighting over illegal tariffs placed on imported steel.
- A small, impoverished nation needs funds to build a nationwide school system.
- A border dispute has led to a major refugee crisis requiring emergency aid and a diplomatic solution.

Step Three: Organizational Cooperation. Have students return to their desks, and then come up with a final scenario where multiple organizations might be involved. Here's an example:

Post-Tsunami Recovery in Zanzibel Island

Imagine the small island nation of Zanzibel, a major exporter of high-end specialized wood products, is devastated by a massive tsunami. The disaster wipes out coastal towns, destroys most export facilities, and collapses the local economy. Which organizations would be called upon to help and what areas would they be able to help in?

SEL connection: Students may have connections or experiences in areas of the world that are currently or previously experiencing dangerous conditions, crises, or war. You may even have students who represent different sides of conflicts in different areas of the world. Sensitivity to different perspectives and trauma-inflicting triggers is critical.

What In the World Is a Feedback Loop?

The concept of a feedback loop is central to systems thinking and understanding complex global issues. It moves students beyond simple linear cause-and-effect to seeing issues as self-reinforcing cycles.

A feedback loop is a process in a system where the outputs (results) of an action are "fed back" and become new inputs (causes), creating a self-reinforcing cycle. In the context of global systems, this means that solving a problem in one area can create a benefit that speeds up progress, or a crisis in one area can trigger a related crisis that makes the original one worse.

There are two primary types of feedback loops:

Positive (Reinforcing) Feedback Loops a positive feedback loop drives a system *further and further* in the same direction, either for better or for worse. It *amplifies* the initial change.

Example (Worse): Climate Change and Polar Ice.

Start: Global temperatures rise (the input).

Action: Ice melts, exposing dark ocean water (the output).

Feedback: Dark water absorbs more solar heat than reflective ice (the new input).

Result: This absorption causes temperatures to rise *even faster*, leading to *more* melting, in a runaway cycle.

Example (Better): Economic Development and Education.

Start: A developing country receives a small loan to build a school.

Action: More children are educated, leading to a more skilled workforce.

Feedback: The skilled workforce attracts foreign investment and starts more businesses.

Result: The nation's economy grows, allowing the government to invest *more* in education and infrastructure.

Negative (Balancing) Feedback Loops A negative feedback loop works to stabilize, correct, or reverse an initial change. It acts like a thermostat, trying to bring the system back to a desired state of balance (equilibrium).

Example: The Global Oil Market.

Start: The price of oil is very high (the **input**).

Action: Consumers drive less, use more efficient cars, and switch to alternative energy (the **output**).

Feedback: The reduced demand for oil leads to a drop in the global oil price (the **new input**).

Result: The price drops, making alternative energy less competitive, and the system attempts to balance itself.

Teaching the Concept of Feedback Loops

This could definitely be a stand-alone lesson after you completed the lesson above. Have students re-examine the Crisis Scenarios from Skill NGA3 and identify a potential feedback loop:

For the collapsing currency scenario, a positive feedback loop could involve panic selling of the currency driving the value down further, which triggers more panic selling.

For the border dispute and refugee crisis, a positive feedback loop could involve lack of diplomatic solution leading to more conflict, which creates more refugees, which then overwhelms humanitarian resources, leading to greater instability and thus more conflict.

Skill NGA4: *Multi-Level Governance Understanding: I can differentiate between the different jurisdictions and responsibilities of local, state, and national governments, and explain how these governments interact with each other and with international bodies to address national and global issues.*

For this skill, we will look at organizations and treaties that help to craft policy around events that serve as existential crises

TABLE 8.3 Health and Humanitarian Organizations

Organization/Agreement	*Acronym*	*Primary Role and Global Significance*
World Health Organization (Part of the UN)	WHO	Directs and coordinates international health efforts, especially during global emergencies like pandemics, and sets health standards
Centers for Disease Control	CDC	The U.S. national public health agency; provides scientific data, guidance, funding, and expertise to state/local health departments
United Nations High Commissioner for Refugees (Part of the UN)	UNHRC	Protects refugees, forcibly displaced communities, and stateless people, and to assist in finding long-term solutions, such as voluntary repatriation, local integration, or resettlement.

that transcend national borders. They are often unpopular, mostly because the subjects that they address are nightmare-inducing scenarios. The United States contributes to each of these organizations, and leads the CDC which supplies information to other bodies in the world (Table 8.3).

Health and Humanitarian Organizations

The lesson connected to these groups has a real-life connection, that of the COVID-19 pandemic of 2020.

Give students the background of COVID-19. It's possible that the students you teach will no longer have memory of what happened in the first days of the pandemic, so it's important to give them a solid base of information:

The COVID-19 threat was caused by the novel coronavirus, SARS-CoV-2, which emerged in late 2019 and spread into a full-scale global pandemic by early 2020. It began in the Wuhan province of China and rapidly spread to Europe and then other parts of the world. It was a virus that the human species had not encountered and was causing widespread death and disability due to the body's reaction to the virus. No known cure was available and no vaccine had yet been developed. It led to a multi-pronged crisis at the international level.

Health Crisis: *The virus was highly contagious and led to massive illness and death globally, overwhelming healthcare systems and forcing widespread, unprecedented public health measures like mandatory lockdowns, mask mandates, and mass testing.*

Security and Humanitarian Crisis: *The panic triggered a rapid breakdown in international cooperation. Countries closed borders, leading to the largest restriction on movement in decades, which directly impacted vulnerable populations, challenging the fundamental mandates of organizations like the UNHCR.*

Essentially, the threat wasn't just a biological one; it was a total breakdown of global stability that challenged every type of international organization.

Have students research what the responses were from the World Health Organization, the UNHRC, and the CDC, and how international organizations and the US responded to the medical emergency. Then have them evaluate the response of the three organizations/agreements. Since this was a brand new illness, were the responses justified? Why or why not?

WHO	What was their first official declaration? What initial advice did they give regarding travel and border closures? What was the major criticism leveled against the WHO's early response?
UNHCR	How did the rapid closure of national borders immediately impact the agency's ability to protect refugees? Why did the closure of official land borders lead to new dangers for displaced people?
CDC	What is the CDC's primary domestic function (providing guidance, data, and funding)? How did the CDC use its authority regarding quarantine and travel restrictions (a specific federal power) in the early days of the outbreak?
WHO vs. CDC	How did the guidance from the WHO (international) sometimes conflict with the actions or mandates of the CDC (national/federal), especially regarding testing protocols or travel bans (Table 8.4)?

TABLE 8.4 Federalism and National Emergencies

Jurisdiction	*National/Federal (CDC/HHS)*	*State Government (State Health Dept.)*	*Local Government (City/County Health Dept.)*
Primary Role	Scientific guidance, funding, vaccine procurement.	Implementing, enforcing, and modifying federal guidance.	Direct service, public outreach, testing sites, contact tracing.
Mask Mandates	Issued *recommendations* and mandates on federal property.	Issued (or prohibited) *statewide* mandates.	Issued local mandates (e.g., in schools, city buildings).
Testing/ Data	Developed initial test kits; collected & distributed national data.	Managed testing sites; reported data to the CDC.	Operated community testing sites; conducted contact tracing
Funding	Provided grants (e.g., through the CDC Foundation) to lower levels.	Allocated grants to cities/counties for public health programs.	Used funds to hire surge staff (e.g., contact tracers).

You can give students a blank chart and then fill it in with them, answering questions as they go. Then consider having discussion questions such as:

1. *The CDC provides* ***guidance****, but State/Local health departments handle* ***enforcement****. How did the lack of a single, unified federal mandate (beyond specific quarantine powers) create different outcomes and public confusion across states?*
2. *The CDC relies on data from State and Local departments. What happens to the national response (and the CDC's recommendations) when state and local cooperation is inconsistent or politically motivated? (This highlights the* fragility *of federal systems in a crisis).*
3. *How did the* ***UNHCR's*** *struggle with border closures mirror the challenges of state governors who tried to impose travel*

restrictions on people coming from other U.S. states? (Both highlight the tension between local safety and the right to free movement).

Then have students answer these questions individually, and then discuss them by table or pairs:

- **Global vs. Domestic Messaging:** The WHO and the CDC are both health authorities, yet their messaging often diverged or was perceived differently due to national politics. The WHO's primary mandate is global coordination and providing standards for its 193 member states. The CDC's mandate is protecting U.S. health and security. How do these different scopes of responsibility naturally lead to different policy recommendations?
- **Resource Flow:** Trace the flow of resources: The Federal government (via the CDC) provided billions in relief. How did the *success* of the response in your community depend on the effectiveness of the State government's ability to coordinate with Local health agencies?
- **Humanitarian Crisis:** The UNHCR's work was disrupted by countries closing borders. Explain how the domestic debate over who had the authority to close state borders to travelers from other states (a National vs. State question) reflects the fundamental conflict of a global health crisis: prioritizing sovereign security over free movement.

Finally, have students put it all together with an opinion and justification. This could be an exit ticket but with a little bit of expansion, it could also be a five paragraph essay question:

Given that COVID-19 was a brand new illness, were the responses of the WHO, UNHCR, and the domestic governments (Federal/State/Local) justified? Why or why not? (Students must use examples of both cooperation and friction between at least two levels of governance in their final evaluation).

Time for Reflection: *Though the students you will be teaching may not have any working memory connected to the pandemic, it will be fresh in your mind. Take some time to reflect on how you can teach this lesson in a way that does not trigger emotional reactions for you. You might also want to consider notifying the parents of your students that you are teaching this lesson to describe Multi-Level Governance Understanding so that when your students go home and talk about it, their parents aren't caught off-guard.*

Skill NGA5: *Global Problem-Solving Approaches: I can propose and evaluate different approaches to addressing national and global challenges, considering diverse perspectives, ethical implications, and effectiveness of certain strategies.*

The Challenge of Collective Security

Your students have learned that the world operates through complex systems (NGA3) and is managed by layers of government and international bodies (NGA4). But what happens when diplomacy fails, stability collapses, and global security is threatened?

This final skill moves us past analysis and into action. Global problems such as regional conflict, nuclear proliferation, or state failure cannot be solved by any single country. They require collective security and shared strategy, which means diverse nations with different priorities must come together to craft a single, effective solution. This is where the challenge of Global Problem-Solving lies: balancing military power with diplomacy, local needs with international law, and immediate humanitarian concerns with long-term stability.

This lesson focuses on the organizations that deal with the world's most difficult choices—those related to security and defense policy. Students will examine how major security alliances (NATO), regional political blocs (AU), and crucial global treaties (NPT) operate not in isolation, but in concert, to prevent global threats. The students' task is to step into the role of a diplomat and craft a comprehensive stabilization plan, forcing them to confront the ethical trade-offs, diverse political perspectives, and strategic limitations inherent in global governance.

The Global Security Council Simulation will help students navigate a new area of world politics, that of security and defense policy. Begin with this chart of international organizations and agreements (Table 8.5).

Have students research these three organizations and treaties. Once they have a good knowledge, then assign them into three groups, each group representing one of the organizations. Then present them with the following scenario (or one like it):

The fictional state of Tenere in Africa has recently ended a brutal civil war. The country is split between two main factions, and its infrastructure is destroyed. The primary concern is that the country's former, limited civilian nuclear research facility is now unsecured, raising fears of its materials falling into the wrong hands.

The three organizations must cooperate to draft a single "Pact for Stabilization and Future Growth."

Have each group prepare a structured plan for peace with action plans and timelines. Then have them come together to negotiate the points in the plans together into one comprehensive whole, with action steps, timelines, and which organization

TABLE 8.5 International Organizations and Agreements

Organization/ Agreement	*Acronym*	*Primary Role and Global Significance*
North Atlantic Treaty Organization	NATO	A collective security alliance that coordinates military defense and strategic policy, primarily among North American and European states.
African Union	AU	Promotes unity, solidarity, and cooperation among African states and plays a major role in conflict resolution and peace support on the continent.
Nuclear Non-Proliferation Treaty	NPT	An international treaty whose objective is to prevent the spread of nuclear weapons and weapons technology.

will be responsible for each result. Then have them present it by reading it out in total. Consider having them sign it like an official document as well.

Understanding and Appreciating Our Military as Citizens

Another way that we can empower students as citizens is to provide opportunities for them to learn about the various branches of the United States military and their roles in supporting our democracy and ways of life. In addition to the three branches of government, the formation and responsibilities of our military are essential for citizens to understand how our country is run and who is defending our freedoms.

> Each year we attend ceremonies at local military cemeteries that honor and respect those who have served our country. In December, we place wreaths and/or read their names and thank them for their service. In May, we place flags at the graves of soldiers and their spouses to remember them for Memorial Day. I feel strongly that this is an important experience for everyone to acknowledge and show gratitude for citizens who stepped up for our country (Figure 8.1).
>
> —Denise

Conclusion: This Is A Lot—But It Is the Whole Enchilada?

This chapter, focusing on National and Global Awareness, is arguably the most complex. It requires students to adopt systems thinking and to juggle a high volume of new organizations and vocabulary. Consequently, it will require the most careful scaffolding for younger learners and those with special learning needs.

FIGURE 8.1 Laying wreaths on the graves of service members.

> I love the Mark Twain quote: travel is fatal to prejudice, bigotry, and narrow-mindedness. Short of international travel, I love experiences that put students into new situations (reading novels, international pen pals). I often did current events projects, which I think students mostly saw as a checkbox instead of a learning opportunity. I tried having students read the cover of the *NY Times* when we got the print paper and then switching to app-based round ups (what you missed this weekend-type content) that students could read or listen to. I also encouraged them to find three news accounts that they enjoyed to follow on social media, which I think was probably the most successful approach for embedding reputable news into their daily information diet.
>
> — Paige, teacher librarian

For middle school or foundational classes, you can focus solely on Skill NGA1 (Global Systems Analysis) using the United Nations as the central topic. Learning the purpose of the UN and the core missions of three or four of its major operational arms may be the full competency goal. (Adding a Model UN scenario for students would help here to have them work through the aspects of crafting legislation through multiple lenses and with an eye to multiple causes and effects).

For high school, teaching the full competency is appropriate, using the UN as the anchor before layering on the IMF, World Bank, and WTO for complexity. The emphasis should shift from *identifying* organizations to analyzing their interactions and the ripple effects.

Ultimately, the difficulty of this chapter only underscores its necessity. The goal of this competency framework *Portrait of a Citizen* is to cultivate responsible citizens. In a world defined by pandemics, economic interdependence, and climate crises, citizenship can no longer be limited to national borders.

By teaching students to identify the complex systems that deliver their phones or cookies, and the international bodies that try to manage those systems, we equip them to understand that their everyday decisions—what they consume, and for whom they vote—are inherently multilateral and global. This chapter ensures that our students graduate with the "wide-angle look" necessary to navigate, and ultimately contribute to, the whole interconnected world.

> For teachers hoping to nurture the skills of national and global awareness I would urge them to create concrete opportunities for students to learn from and become curious of each other—seeking to learn about their classmates' stories, histories, and cultures. And I would think about ways to incorporate student passions and interests in class. Our students care so deeply about their communities; they just might not yet have the skills to effectively advocate, and this creates a great opportunity in classrooms to develop authentic civic projects that are student-led and locally focused.
>
> —Jessica, teacher and author

Spotlight on Sources

The United Nations: https://www.un.org/en The actual site where your students can research and get more information on the organs and organizations.

Model UN https://www.un.org/en/mun Also through the UN, but with an eye toward the simulations.

References

Merriam-Webster, Incorporated. (n.d.). *Merriam-Webster.com dictionary*. Retrieved November 23, 2025, from https://www.merriam-webster.com/

Roosevelt, F. D. (1945, January 6). *Annual message to the congress: The state of the union* [Radio address transcript]. The American Presidency Project. Retrieved November 23, 2025, from https://www.irs.gov/individuals/get-transcript; https://www.irs.gov/individuals/get-transcript

9

Differences Celebrated

We All Live in a Yellow Submarine

Introduction

The modern world is defined by constant interaction with people around the world. We are no longer limited to connecting only with those who look like us, worship like us, or grew up in the same neighborhoods. Our schools, workplaces, communities, and digital spaces are rich tapestries of different ages, cultural backgrounds, and ideological beliefs. Further, we interact with people whom we will never meet, in TikTok videos, social media posts, and online forums or classrooms. We also interact with non-people like trolls or bots that are designed to invoke outrage or fear.

This chapter argues that for students to be successful citizens, it's not enough for them to simply tolerate diversity; they must celebrate it. When a group brings together unique perspectives, including differing political opinions, the resulting solutions are stronger, more creative, and more equitable. They must also learn not to feed the trolls. This final competency serves as the capstone for your entire civic matrix. These kids we teach are *already* global citizens; it's time for them to celebrate their differences and celebrate each other.

DOI: 10.4324/9781003746614-9

The Interwoven Fabric of Citizenship

The good news is that these skills aren't new; in fact, they are interwoven into the previous chapters, and most likely into the work that we do every day in all of our classrooms. Here's a snapshot on where the competency of Difference Celebrated overlaps with the other competencies in the book.

Civic Knowledge. To truly understand Historical Contextualization or analyze Current Events, you must recognize that different groups have radically different experiences and interpretations of the same facts.

Community Engagement. Accomplishing Collaborative Problem-Solving is impossible unless you first use skills to understand the diverse needs and assets of your community. Taking Action must be guided by Inclusive Collaboration to ensure the change is equitable. There will be different opinions about what solutions might be possible; all of those voices are valid and need to be recognized.

Ethical Decision-Making. This entire competency hinges on Differences Celebrated. You cannot effectively engage in Value Recognition or practice Empathetic Reasoning without the Active Listening required to understand opposing ethical positions, competing values, or momentary suspension of long-held values. Additionally, reaching Compromise and Consensus is the practical result of successfully navigating ideological differences.

Critical Thinking. The core skill of Bias and Perspective Recognition is powerfully reinforced here. By engaging directly with diverse individuals, you are forced to confront both your explicit biases (attitudes and beliefs you are consciously aware of) and, more importantly, your implicit biases (unconscious stereotypes or attitudes that affect your understanding and actions). This process allows you to directly challenge your own pre-existing assumptions, thereby elevating your ability to evaluate information based on its source and context, not just whether it aligns with your comfort zone.

National and Global Awareness. The ability to propose Global Problem-Solving Approaches requires understanding that nations have vastly different priorities rooted in their unique histories and cultures. This provides the interpersonal tools needed to succeed in global diplomacy.

This chapter is the point where you take all your knowledge and skills and apply them through the most essential civic lens: respectful human interaction. It asks students to move beyond passive acceptance and engage in active, reflective practice. It ensures that your students graduate with the emotional intelligence and collaborative spirit necessary to build, not just reside in, a functioning democracy.

SEL connection: This competency is the perfect time to include positive and active listening lessons, as well as conflict resolution skills—in both online forums and in-person situations. It is clear that *listening to learn* (rather than *listening to respond*) is a skill that may have to be explicitly taught, especially in situations in which participants disagree.

Shifting the *What* to *How*

You might be asking yourself: if this competency is so interwoven into the other chapters, why is it a stand-alone chapter, and why is it the last competency?

Every other competency focuses on an objective task or external knowledge, or the WHAT in a lesson. Civic Knowledge and National and Global Awareness focus on *what* the learner knows (facts, global systems, governmental structures). Community Engagement focuses on *what* the learner does (identifying needs, implementing action). Critical Thinking focuses on *what* the learner analyzes (information, bias, propaganda). Ethical Decision-Making focuses on *what* principles the learner applies (values, ethical frameworks).

Differences Celebrated is the only competency that focuses on the internal, relational process, or the HOW. Navigating deep ideological and political disagreements (a core goal of this chapter) is the most difficult aspect of citizenship and requires explicit, dedicated training. While students might identify media bias in a Critical Thinking lesson, the Differences Celebrated chapter forces them to practice the emotional labor of engaging with a perspective that challenges their core values in order to intentionally reflect on *how* a political viewpoint different from their own forces them to change or nuance their thinking.

This chapter will help students to practice finding common ground and foster positive relationships with people whose opinions they fundamentally oppose, distinguishing between the person and the policy. This dedicated space ensures these critical skills aren't just assumed but actively developed. We can't infer that students already have these skills anymore, and we need to ensure that we provide safe spaces for them to practice them.

This chapter provides the final, vital test of application. It measures the student's ability to transition from a student of civics to an active, responsible, and inclusive practitioner of citizenship. It is the moment where the intellectual work of the previous chapters becomes integrated with the necessary human element, proving they have the emotional intelligence and interpersonal rigor required to sustain a healthy democracy.

Time to Reflect: *What are your successes when it comes to celebrating differences in your classroom? What are successes when it comes to celebrating differences in your school? What may be evidence of these successes?*

The Sixth Competency: Differences Celebrated

Differences Celebrated: The learner works with people of different ages and backgrounds. They celebrate unique perspectives and lived experiences by actively listening, expanding their beliefs, and making connections with others.

Associated Skills

To achieve this competency, students will develop the ability to (Table 9.1):

TABLE 9.1 Skills of Differences Celebrated

DC1	**Inclusive Collaboration** I can work in diverse groups, showing respect for others and contributions from individuals of different ages, cultural backgrounds, and lived experiences.
DC2	**Active Listening and Empathy** I can actively listen to and strive to understand perspectives and lived experiences that differ from my own and avoid making assumptions based on previously held beliefs.
DC3	**Expanding Beliefs and Open-Mindedness** I can articulate how interacting with diverse groups has allowed me to challenge or expand my beliefs, understandings, or prior assumptions.
DC4	**Bridging Divides and Making Connections** I can initiate and foster positive relationships with individuals from various backgrounds and contribute to a sense of community across differences.
DC5	**Honoring Diverse Action** I can promote and celebrate diverse pathways for civic action and engagement, recognizing and valuing contributions for all community members.

Key Vocabulary from Merriam-Webster (n.d.)

Diversity: The presence of differences among a group, including varied cultural backgrounds, ages, experiences, and political or ideological beliefs.

Empathy: The ability to understand and share the feelings and reasoning behind another person's perspective, even if you fundamentally disagree with their opinion.

Perspective: A specific point of view or way of looking at a situation, often shaped by an individual's personal experiences, culture, and political orientation or core values.

Assumption: A thing accepted as true or certain without proof, often applied to stereotypes about others' backgrounds, motivations, or political affiliations

Inclusion: The practice of ensuring all people, regardless of their differences or political opinions, feel respected, valued, and fully integrated into the community or discussion.

Skill 1. Inclusive Collaboration: *I can work in diverse groups, showing respect for others and integrating contributions from individuals of different ages, cultural backgrounds, and lived experiences.*

Schools get a bad rap these days. What if we could get members of the community to come into the schools and interact with the students to see all the good that is happening? Would those people then be more likely to vote yes on the school budget? Would they be more likely to go to the school's football game? These lessons serve a dual purpose; they teach students inclusive collaboration, but they also are genuine acts of community-building, and intergenerational understanding. They are designed to break down the barrier between "town" and "gown" and have students work with community members, young and old, to design ways of learning from each other.

Lost Skills or Local Lore Guide

Have students identify areas of local, non-recorded knowledge that is often lost between generations (local recipes, slang from a previous era, how to fix an appliance without using YouTube, the location of unmarked historical locations or landmarks). Students then work with a local organization, whether it be a VFW, senior center, or retirement village, to find intergenerational partners to serve as Subject Matter Experts on the topic. The Subject Matter Experts can go to the school or the students can go on a brief field trip to interview the Subject Matter Experts. Students will serve as recorders, curators, and editors of the information.

The final product can be a professional-quality published resource, possibly a website, a printed book, or a video series around the chosen topic. The students will work to document, organize, and market the mentor's knowledge, ensuring that the contribution is celebrated and preserved for the community at large.

The final publication or launch event becomes the platform where mentors are honored as co-creators, seeing their knowledge being turned into a modern, accessible asset for the community.

Building an Interactive Community Map

Students plan and build a digital map (using StoryMaps or something similar link at the end of the chapter) showcasing historical points of interest, including spots that might not be officially recognized.

Mentors from the community can be brought into school to provide the content (oral histories, memories, locations, and context) while students provide the technical expertise (digital mapping, photography, interviewing and editing the audio clips). The project cannot be completed without the knowledge and collaboration from both groups with different backgrounds. The finished map is presented to the historical society or town government, establishing the students as valuable partners in preserving history and providing the mentors with a lasting, digital legacy.

Skill DC2. Active Listening and Empathy: *I can actively listen to and strive to understand perspectives and lived experiences that differ from my own and avoid making assumptions based on previously held beliefs.*

Oral Histories for Community Members

This lesson uses a structured interview process to ensure students actively listen to and respect the unique perspectives of older community members by conducting, synthesizing, and presenting oral histories gathered from older mentors.

Partner with a local senior center, veterans group, or school alumni association. Students work in groups of three to interview a mentor on a specific civic theme that has changed over time (such as "The History of Voting in Our Town," "Experiences with Early Civil Rights Movements," "Community Response to the Last Major Crisis," or "My Experience with September 11, 2001").

Students ask the community member a series of questions and the community member shares his or her experiences. Students can record or video the interview. Then students compile the data from the interview and create a composition on the event and that person's experience. It's recommended that a picture be taken of the person.

Students then develop a museum-like display with each person and their experience, perhaps with written and/or audio recordings of the interview. The exhibit could go on display at the local library or senior center. There could even be an opening night with refreshments and remarks.

> I would encourage teachers to reflect on all the many strengths students bring to their classrooms and communities and then figure out ways to intentionally nurture those strengths as part of their curriculum and class projects. My students have so many strengths that they bring to our classroom and our communities. I think sometimes some people—and institutions—think about our students with a deficit-based mindset: focusing on what they don't have. Maybe they're still mastering English, maybe they're still struggling with how academics are taught here versus in their home country, may be they are facing other challenges. But it's so important to remember and invest in all the powerful strengths that our students bring to our classrooms. My students are cultural and linguistic navigators for their families. They bring a wealth of knowledge and experience having lived in multiple countries and cultures, and they show tremendous amounts of grit and determination as they navigate a new school system, a new community, a new country. In journeying to this country, they've often become masters at negotiation, problem-solving, and teamwork. Here, they're creating new friendships and they're learning new languages. They are deeply generous towards each other. They bring their determination, creativity, compassion, and courage to our classroom and our community.
>
> – Jessica, teacher and author

BEST Practices to Meet Diverse Needs of Learners

- **Bridge** (English/multilingual learners): This activity may bring a lot of stress for your multilingual learner. Consider having them interview someone in their home language if possible, or pairing them with a strong pair of English speakers who can help. They also may view or research the history of the area from another perspective if applicable (such as that of indigenous peoples, immigrants who have come to the area, people of color, or anyone else with whom they may find representation).
- **Expand** (gifted students): Making connections for your students to the history here will really benefit them to make connections across the curriculum. These students may want to interview people who they think may have opposing perspectives on the history or culture of the town; they can then set up their display with a compare/contrast lens.
- **Support** (students with learning challenges or differences): Going over the questions with your students in advance and having them practice with each other will help greatly with this activity. In addition, teaching them to extend "off script" might be a way to show them how they can follow up on a question. This might need some modelling between two teachers or a teacher and a willing community member.
- **Teamwork:** Giving students different tasks within the team will help make the product stronger. If one person is in charge of asking the questions, one is in charge of taking care of the recording, one is in charge of listening for opportunities for follow up questions, etc., it keeps each child focused on their task and not overly anxious that they are missing something.

Spotlight on Newcomers: If you have a large number of newcomers, consider having them tell their immigration story as a means of oral history. Have students interview each other about their immigration story and the hardships they faced as they arrived and now live in a new country. This could be a powerful way of connecting across your classes. Some students may not want to share their personal stories for whatever reason; they can research primary documents or interview others if they prefer that.

Many cultures and languages focus on a strong oral history to share stories and pass down traditions through the generations. These types of activities—such as interviewing local community members or listening to podcasts highlighting firsthand accounts—may be powerful ways that students connect with their own family traditions. We often focus on the written history and its importance; this may be a time in which oral artifacts shine.

Time to Reflect: *Reflect on your own perspectives: Are there certain groups that you may feel less empathy for than others? Are there languages or cultures that you may value more than others? What can you do as a human to examine your own potential biases and make small changes in both your perceptions and your behavior?*

Skill 3. Expanding Beliefs and Open-Mindedness: *I can articulate how interacting with diverse groups has allowed me to challenge or expand my beliefs, understandings, or prior assumptions.*

So today my American history class took a test on the 13 colonies, mercantilism, the triangular trade, the Enlightenment and the Great Awakening. Brings you

> right back, huh? But my class is in an international school. My students in that particular class come from Nigeria, China, Brazil, Mexico, Vietnam, Thailand, Uzbekistan and Kazakhstan. The essay question was "How does slavery contradict ideals of the Enlightenment such as liberty, equality, and justice?" A no brainer, right? But some of these kids come from countries that still have slavery. I looked around the class as they were taking the test and thought to myself, "Wow, imagine if this made a real difference, if these kids took this home and fostered a change."
>
> —Anonymous teacher

This skill is closely aligned with the previous chapter on Ethical Decision-Making, especially if you are already using the reflective journal and open-ended reflective questions. The question here is: how do you allow a student to do the emotional work of changing their own mind on a topic? The difference between this skill and the skills of Ethical Decision-Making is that students have external interactions with people, not just ideas, documents, videos, or historical events.

The Assumption Audit

One way to foster active growth for students when they interact with different groups and generations is to do work with an Assumption Audit, where students explore their own assumptions and biases *before* entering into a conversation or interaction, and then actively listening for contradictions to their previously held belief. This takes a lot of scaffolding but the cumulative effects could be phenomenal.

Pre-Activity, Assumption Exploration: Before students engage in an interaction with someone of a different generation or a senior citizen, like in the oral histories or intergenerational collaboration earlier in this chapter, have students write the answer to these questions:

What is a general assumption I have about this group of people? (Answers might include something like "Senior Citizens don't understand technology" or "People on the opposite political side don't see reason.")

What is a closely held belief I have about this topic that I believe is universally true? Answers might include something like, "Police officers make people scared" or "Cities are dangerous places."

During Activity, Active Listening for Disruptive Quotes: When students interact with that group of people or in a certain place, prepare them to actively listen for disrupting quotes. Disrupting quotes are quotes that challenge their assumptions or beliefs. Have students note these quotes or have them work in teams where one person is in charge of recording the disruptive quotes.

Post Activity Audit: Have students revisit their initial assumptions or beliefs and also their disruptive quotes. Allow them time to discuss how the disruptive quotes might have changed their viewpoints. Then encourage them to journal about it. A good prompt might be, "I used to believe _________, but then _______________ said this_____________________, and now my thinking is________________________." This is going to take some time, but could be so rich for their mindset and for the subsequent interactions between students and either the original person, or the next representative from that group.

SEL connection: Assumptions are often a barrier to authentic interactions and connections among stakeholders or peers. By scaffolding this activity with discussions of assumptions that are meaningful to your students' lives—with intentional consideration of all perspectives—you can establish a culture in which assumptions can be respectfully questioned or even challenged.

BEST Practices to Meet Diverse Needs of Learners

- **Bridge** (English/multilingual learners): Allow students to use graphic organizers (like a T-chart or a Venn diagram) to map out the "Old Assumption" and the "New Learning" visually before writing the final articulation. If they are writing about a cultural belief, allow them to discuss it first in their home language with a partner, if possible, to clarify the nuance before translating their insight into English.
- **Expand** (gifted students): Encourage these students to identify an assumption they hold that is based on a **strong, logical argument** (not a stereotype). They can then seek out the counter-argument's human element. The final articulation should explain not only *how* their assumption was broken, but *why* the emotional or experiential evidence they gathered outweighed the purely logical or data-driven position they previously held.
- **Support** (students with learning challenges or differences): Explicitly provide sentence stems for the reflection phase. This scaffolding helps structure the abstract idea of a "belief change" into a concrete, evidence-based response.
- **Teamwork:** Students can design interview questions to engage others in this type of reflection. Interviews may be recorded or students may take notes to share with the class.

Time to Reflect: *Think about the most difficult conversation you had with a family member or colleague whose core political or social beliefs differed fundamentally from your own. What was the assumption you had about them before the conversation, and what specific thing did they say or do that forced you to slightly adjust or complicate that assumption? What emotional resistance did you have to overcome to change your mind?*

Skill DC4. Bridging Divides and Making Connections: *I can initiate and foster positive relationships with individuals from various backgrounds and contribute to a sense of community across differences.*

This is a tough topic, especially in a polarized political environment. It's also going to take a lot of slow building This isn't a "one and done" lesson, but more like a series of lessons where students can talk to, and learn from, each other.

One way to bridge the divide between two different political views is the "Reflective Restatement" protocol, where students learn to listen to each other and then reflect back what the other person is saying. This will take some modelling, most helpfully with another teacher, to show how it works.

> We foster civil discourse by laying the groundwork that people will have different opinions than you and that is great—but to be respectful and polite to them when having these discussions. It is good to challenge the opinions of others, but it has to be done with ground rules and in a mature, respectful way.
>
> —Matt, history teacher

Common Ground Interviews

Introduce a controversial topic, about which the students might have different opinions. You might even want to put them on the wall with "Strongly Agree" or "Strongly Disagree." Then you can pair students up based upon where they are standing along the line.

Some controversial topics might include (but are not limited to):

- Should certain felonies committed by juveniles (16–17) automatically result in being tried as an adult?
- Should citizens have the right to film police officers during a stop, even if it interferes with the officer's job?
- Should the government require social media companies to actively monitor and delete content deemed "misinformation" about health or elections?

- Should all new cars be required to have technology that can disable the vehicle remotely if a driver has committed a serious offense?
- Should cities be allowed to clear long-term homeless encampments from public parks and sidewalks?
- Should public colleges only offer free tuition to students who commit to working in-state for five years after graduation?
- Should voting be compulsory for all citizens?

Then once students are matched up, have them take turns listening to and then restating each other's opinion. Students will take turns giving their side of the opinion on the controversial topics. The core rule is: The restatement is considered successful only when the original speaker confirms, "Yes, that's exactly what I meant." It is helpful, sometimes, to have a "talking stick" or something similar. That is, a visible symbol of the person's right to talk. When the person is talking, they are holding the talking stick, and the other is listening. Then, they switch and pass the stick.

BEST practices: Sentence stems, sentence frames, time to prepare, and time to research the topics may be beneficial for many students.

Challenging Commonality or "Bridging the Divide"

Students do not need to agree on the topic, but challenge them to find *something* they agree upon during this conversation. When the exercise is over, encourage students to report out on the things they agreed upon and then have them reflect on the exercise itself. It is likely that this activity will be very new to them, they are not discussing to win, they are discussing to understand.

Consider doing this before a holiday and give students the option of trying this out at their family dinner table, perhaps with a relative with whom they do not agree, or encourage students to talk about this method at the holidays with their family and offer to try it out together.

Skill DC5. Honoring Diverse Action: *I can promote and celebrate diverse pathways for civic action and engagement, recognizing and valuing contributions from all community members.*
Your students will, upon graduation, undoubtedly be able to explain various pathways for civic participation and advocacy, especially if you, your department, or your district follow the *Portrait of a Citizen* Framework. How do we as educators instill in them the core belief that one of the key aspects of graduation is going out into the world as informed, connected empathetic, thoughtful citizens ready to take on the challenges that this world and nation face?

Voter Registration as Part of Senior Week

We have big celebrations for students when they graduate. We have walk-throughs where students wear their caps and gowns. There are proms, awards ceremonies, and cap decoration ceremonies. Some schools have drive-by parades. What if we included a part of Senior Week where they also registered to vote? What if we made it a part of Senior Week and it became a part of the whole fabric of the week? Since you are *already* celebrating seniors that week, why not make it a normal coming-of-age celebration?

> Last year we participated with the League of Women Voters to start a school project among our seniors to educate them on how to register to vote and how to vote at the polls. The school gave us a day to educate the seniors on how to cast their votes before the election and this was very impactful as 30 students registered to vote, and the overall student feedback reflected a renewed enthusiasm for the voting process.
>
> —Matt, history teacher

In *The Power of Moments* by Heath and Heath (2017), they identify four key elements to make certain moments extraordinary: *Elevation, Insight, Pride, and Connection.*

Elevation: Moments that break the routine and stand out from the ordinary. Don't make the registration to vote just a table in the cafeteria. Elevate it to their first official duty as high school graduates. Have a "Pledge to Participate" station with pictures of famous civil rights leaders, or other patriotic symbols. Have students read a civic pledge or "citizenship charter" as part of their registration.

Insight: Moments of insight or epiphany that change how we see the world. Invite a local official to give brief remarks on the journey that they are about to take and the important step they are making in becoming key parts of democracy. Talk about what one person can do by showing local elections and the difference of just a few votes.

Pride: Moments of achievement, courage or recognition that catch us at our best. Frame the moment as they are ready, they have been trained, and they are going into the world to create change. Acknowledge that voting often means choosing between imperfect options or standing up for a value that is not popular. Frame the act of thoughtful registration and subsequent voting as an act of civic courage and integrity. Immediately after registration, award a distinctive **VOTE** pin to be worn with the cap and gown. This is a visible symbol of their new status, equal in pride to any academic honor.

Connection: Moments that strengthen our bonds with others, such as deep experiences or shared conversations. Invite parents to be a part of the ceremony, and have a picture of all the new registrants under a Class of 20– banner with the words WE VOTE! You can also have a Selfie Frame with the same words and encourage your students to upload it to their social media.

By weaving the four elements of extraordinary moments into the voter registration process, you transform it from a procedural step into a memorable, meaningful "Civic Commitment Ceremony" that instills the core belief: graduation is the beginning of your lifelong contribution.

Focus on... Some of our students cannot register to vote either because of their documentation or status in this country or for whatever other reason. We still want them to participate in this very important piece of activism—albeit in a different way. We can provide choices of ways that they can "Rock the Vote" themselves, even if they cannot cast their own ballot. These students can engage in letter-writing campaigns to elected officials or creating educational materials to encourage others to vote. They can research issues or court cases that resonate with them (*DACA*, *Lau* v. *Nichols*, *Plyler* v. *Doe*, *Brown* v. *Board of Education*, diverse paths to citizenship) and educate others on them through a lens of a personal perspective. Broader definitions of impactful civic engagement may also include educating the school community on some of the current policies or issues that surround the elections and documenting the ways local government officials are engaging with community members.

The First 100 Day Challenge

Encourage students to make a pledge to do something as a new voter in their first 100 days as high school graduates. That's the time between graduation from high school and the beginning of college. Students could look at their communities and pledge to do something that is new and impactful in their first 100 days after they leave high school. This could include writing a letter to the editor, volunteering at a food bank, helping at the community garden, or going to a town meeting. Have them record their pledge and then compile them for awards night or at the graduation ceremony itself. You can have students say something like, "In my first 100 days as a high school graduate, I vow to ---------."

Conclusion: The Essential Act of Listening

This chapter, "Differences Celebrated," is where you'll begin to see the fruits of your labor, and so will your students! We've shown the entire Portrait of a Citizen Framework including the knowledge, the analysis, and the ethics, which is ultimately translated through the lens of human interaction. The hardest work we ask of our students isn't intellectual; it's relational.

The rigor of this competency lies in recognizing that listening is an active, demanding skill. You cannot effectively analyze a problem until you've done the emotional labor of engaging with the source's lived experience. You cannot successfully achieve a goal until you've successfully bridged a divide to bring diverse people and resources to the table. This competency proves that inclusive collaboration isn't a soft skill; it's the final, non-negotiable test of application for responsible citizenship.

We don't just want our students to tolerate complexity; we want them to actively seek it out, knowing that a community's greatest strength is the creative friction generated by its differences.

This is why we conclude with the Civic Commitment Ceremony and the First 100 Day Challenge. The emotional gravity of these moments like signing a pledge and pinning on a VOTE pin doesn't just celebrate their journey; it seals their intention. It answers the graduate's ultimate question, *What can I do?* by turning abstract skills into a personal declaration of readiness . It's their first, conscious step into a lifelong commitment to informed, empathetic, and accountable participation.

Don't underestimate not only the transformation this will make on your students, but also the transformation this will make on your community. By having students interact with community members, by listening to them and really trying to understand them, you will experience reciprocal gratitude on both sides.

Ultimately, the integrity of our democracy depends not on a perfect set of laws, but on citizens who are willing to listen to learn, celebrate diverse contributions, and remain committed to the ongoing, essential work of human connection. That is the contribution we know our graduates are ready to make.

Spotlight on Sources

StoryMaps on https://storymaps.arcgis.com/

American Exchange Project: https://www.americanexchangeproject.org/ The American Exchange Project is a non-profit based in Boston Massachusetts that provides free, week-long exchanges for high school seniors in the summer after they graduate. The seniors go to a place in America that is radically different from their own, and they learn to live and listen to a whole new group of people. This opportunity would be a great addition to the skill Bridging Divides and Making Connections, as well as a potential pledge for the First 100 Day Challenge.

References

Heath, C., & Heath, D. (2017). *The power of moments: Why certain experiences have extraordinary impact*. Simon & Schuster.

Merriam-Webster, Incorporated. (n.d.). *Merriam-Webster.com dictionary*. Retrieved November 23, 2025, from https://www.merriam-webster.com/

10

How to Use the Matrix

Walking the Path

Introduction

You have spent the previous six chapters exploring the *Portrait of a Citizen* competencies and skills associated with it, designed to help you train a new generation of new citizens as they embark out on their own and start their own lives and their own civic identities. The question is: where do you start and how do you keep the momentum going?

This chapter will help you navigate how to use the Matrix at the individual and departmental level, and possibly how to elevate it up to the district level as well. The matrix isn't just a list of competencies and skills; it's a roadmap for your students' time in secondary education. Each skill is a small step to shepherd your student from passive resident of a community to an active and engaged contributor.

The reality is there is no way that a single teacher can teach all of these skills in a year to a single class, the idea is to do the best you can with what you've got, and when you know better, you do better. Perhaps your class is the year that you will take on a new action civics project, which will take up a large portion of your time. You likely won't also be teaching about the Constitution that year as well and if you *do have the opportunity* to

DOI: 10.4324/9781003746614-10

teach both things in the same class, you likely also won't be teaching about the interconnectedness of international organizations.

There are some skills that can be transferable across all the grades. We can all incorporate more Ethical Decision-Making by allowing students to see a historical issue or era from a number of different sides. Likewise, we want our students to be Critical Thinkers at all times, and skeptical of the things they see, hear, and read. We want our students to celebrate each other's differences, to build bridges, and to expand their beliefs and (occasionally) change their minds!

> I foster civil discourse by making the talking environment safe and friendly. Everyone is allowed to share their respectful and maybe not popular opinions, but always being considerate of their peers. My suggestion to get students to talk is to choose topics that interest the students by getting suggestions, paying attention to what they discuss, and also have talking points or prepared questions, to allow students to have think time before cold calling. This alleviates that anxiety that students feel when not prepared.
>
> —Marie, history/social justice teacher

The true power of the Matrix, then, isn't in slicing and dicing competencies, but in their interconnectedness and stackable skills, in how you can add a little bit to your lessons to make them better. A foreign language teacher once said that learning a foreign language through exposure was like watering sand in the desert, the more water you pour, the more likely something is going to grow. The same is true for incorporating *Portrait of a Citizen* competencies and skills into your day-to-day lessons as buildable skills that make better students who turn into better citizens.

The true power of this framework, and the most effective teaching, occurs not in isolation, but when partners and colleagues intentionally coordinate their instruction. When you look at the vertical alignment and figure out what skills align best with each course, that is when the powerful learning is assured. The Matrix provides the common language for the entire department and school. By sharing the Matrix, you ensure that every single one of the 30 skills is not just *addressed* but systematically scaffolded and assessed across multiple grade levels and courses. This shared responsibility is how to guarantee a complete, integrated civic education for every graduate.

Powerful teaching requires coordinated collaboration among colleagues. So this doesn't need to stop at your department's door, feel free to incorporate the middle and high school together, to vertically align across all the secondary grades, and also to make it a district-wide initiative to have all the secondary social studies teachers work toward the same goal.

The "I Can" Statements

"I Can" statements shift the focus from the teacher to the student. Rather than asking, "What is the teacher teaching?" we are able to ask the question, "What is the student learning and able to do?"

Clarity of Purpose: The I Can statement provides a clarity of purpose. Each statement provides a roadmap of where the student should be by graduation. Some skills will be tackled early and easily, while others will take time and perseverance on both the teacher to provide the lesson and the student to learn it. The skills show mastery. There will be productive struggle for these students, they will grow as they learn, and mature as they grow.

Self-Reflection: I Can statements can also be a tool for self-reflection for the student. Students can review the I Can statements before a lesson to see how they feel they stack up against the statement, and then after the lesson or unit they can review it again. You can start any complex activity by having students review the relevant "I Can" statements. Before a research project, they might check CT1 (Information Analysis and Evaluation). Before a discussion with a community mentor, they review DC2 (Active Listening and Empathy). They can even rate on a 1-5 scale on how well they have mastered the skill before and after the activity.

Common Language: For educators, having a common language is key. The I Can statements can allow for coordinated feedback across classes and the department as a whole. They also can allow for targeted feedback. They allow teachers to give specific, academic feedback rooted in the framework, regardless of the subject area. Instead of saying, "Your research needs to be better," a teacher can say, "To improve, focus on demonstrating CT4 (Conflict of Interest Identification) by tracing the funding of your sources." It's also a great way to communicate with parents so they have a transparent way of knowing what their student is doing and able to accomplish

Vertical Alignment: The I Can statements can be a great entry for vertical alignment across the grades. Asking colleagues what the I Can statement looks like as a 6th grader, versus a 12th grader, and following the goal through the grades can help for coordination and common purpose while mapping curriculum.

Rigor: Rigor in the context of the Matrix is defined not by the difficulty of the content, but by the complexity of the thinking and application required to demonstrate the skill. The need for vertical alignment means that the application of the skill must become more challenging each year. The statement itself stays the same, but the context and tools required to achieve it advance from basic to complex. The I Can statements build rigor because the department works together to make it more challenging and rigorous each year, building upon the work of the previous class or year.

> **BEST practices for all learners:** Teachers sometimes find it challenging to balance between grade-relevant use of academic language and making these statements comprehensible for all learners. If your learners have diverse language and literacy strengths, you can provide the I Can statements connected to the task, concept, or assignment in scaffolded ways. We recommend starting with the most challenging version posted in one color and then a second (or third) version immediately alongside or below it clarifying the statement. All versions say essentially the same thing but access will be embedded into this resource or guide for all learners.

This chart uses three skills from the Critical Thinker (CT) competency to show how the "I Can" statement remains constant, but the context, complexity of application, and assessment tools advance across grade levels (Table 10.1).

The Power of One

Whether your department buys in or not, the Portrait of a Citizen Matrix is a powerful tool for individual rigor and intentionality. You can intentionally stack skills necessary from the Matrix by asking what it is that you want the students to learn, and what you want the students to be able to do.

TABLE 10.1 Examples of Vertical Alignment Across High School Grades

Skill Code & I Can Statement	*9th Grade: World History*	*11th Grade: US History*	*12th Grade: Government/Civics*
CT1: Information Analysis and Evaluation	**Focus:** Evaluating reliability of sources based on origin.	**Focus:** Analyzing the purpose and bias of historical narratives.	**Focus:** Evaluating policy proposals based on data quality and conflicting expert opinion.
I Can: *I can analyze and evaluate the quality of information from diverse sources, including traditional media and social platforms.*	**Application:** Students analyze two differing accounts of the Industrial Revolution (e.g., a factory owner's report vs. a worker's diary) and rate their reliability.	**Application:** Students compare a Progressive Era muckraker article (e.g., Upton Sinclair) to a contemporary textbook account, analyzing how **narrative bias** shapes public opinion.	**Application:** Students evaluate the funding, methodology, and credentials of two opposing economic reports (e.g., CBO vs. a Think Tank) on a proposed tax law.
CT2: Perspective Taking and Empathy	**Focus:** Identifying the motivations and worldviews of historical actors.	**Focus:** Understanding the historical context that drives group perspectives.	**Focus:** Engaging in structured dialogue with stakeholders holding competing values.

(Continued)

TABLE 10.1 (Continued)

Skill Code & I Can Statement	*9th Grade: World History*	*11th Grade: US History*	*12th Grade: Government/Civics*
I Can: *I can understand, describe, and value the multiple perspectives, experiences, and belief systems of others.*	**Application:** Students research and present on the motivations of different groups involved in a conflict (e.g., feudal lords vs. serfs), identifying competing **values**.	**Application:** Students participate in a Socratic Seminar on a controversial event (e.g., Japanese Internment, Vietnam War), arguing from the perspective of a specific historical group (e.g., a veteran, a civil rights leader).	**Application:** Students host a mock community forum on a local zoning issue (e.g., affordable housing), authentically representing the conflicting interests of homeowners, developers, and potential residents.
CT4: Conflict of Interest Identification	**Focus:** Recognizing simple conflicts of interest in source materials.	**Focus:** Tracing complex webs of influence and patronage.	**Focus:** Identifying implicit and systemic conflicts of interest in contemporary policy.
I Can: *I can identify a conflict of interest, bias, or other factors that may compromise the objectivity of a source.*	**Application:** Students read a mercantilist pamphlet and clearly identify the author's economic interest in promoting colonial trade.	**Application:** Students analyze a political cartoon or news report from the Gilded Age, mapping the financial ties between politicians, industrialists, and the press.	**Application:** Students analyze a current piece of legislation (e.g., an environmental bill), tracing the lobbying activity, donor influence, and institutional relationships that could indicate a **systemic conflict of interest**.

Cross-Reference with State Standards: The best way to coordinate the *Portrait of a Citizen* Matrix with the social studies standards of your state is cross-referencing with backward design. This is possible to do by starting with the state standards and then looking to see where they overlap with the Matrix. A faster way to do it is to use a generative AI chatbot of choice.

Ask the chatbot if it is familiar with your state standards, and then feed the Matrix in, and ask where it overlaps and diverges, both explicitly and implicitly. You will find that there are lots of skills that are implicit in the standards, when the Matrix is making them explicit. This is beneficial because you're able to determine the intent of the state standards and how *Portrait of a Citizen* addresses the intent. This process ensures compliance with state mandates while simultaneously guaranteeing the civic depth mandated by the Portrait of a Citizen. The state standard dictates the *topic*, and the Matrix dictates the *cognitive and civic rigor*.

Share the Matrix with Students: Giving students direct access to the Matrix, particularly the "I Can" statements, shifts the dynamic of your classroom by creating immediate transparency and personal accountability. There's no reason they shouldn't know what they are doing or where they are going with the knowledge and skills they are developing. When students know the destination they are more likely to be willing participants in the journey. They will know that these aren't just things they are learning, but they'll understand why they are learning them! This also can provide for goal setting and self-reflection as it provides common vocabulary for them as well. Finally, sharing the whole framework with students reinforces the message that effective citizenship requires a diversity of voices!

Lesson Design for Depth: You can stack your skills into lessons. For example, a lesson on the Constitution would address Civic Knowledge 1, but what if you combined it with another skill? For example, if you combined Civic Knowledge 1 with Ethical Decision-Making (EDM 1: Value Recognition and Prioritization), you could have students identify competing values of the Founders.

Secure Buy-In from Supervisors: Securing commitment from your department head, principal, or district administrators is the final, essential step in elevating the Matrix from a single teacher's tool to a systemic instructional framework. For the powerful teaching promised by vertical alignment to truly take hold, the effort must be officially sanctioned, supported, and resourced. The key to successful buy-in is to translate the idealistic language of "better citizens" into the practical, data-driven language of school improvement, accountability, and rigor. Supervisors need to see the "Portrait" as a solution to existing challenges, not just an add-on.

Operationalize the District's Vision: If your district already has a Portrait of a Learner (PoL) or Portrait of a Graduate (PoG), frame the Matrix not as a new initiative, but as the implementation plan for that vision. Show how your Matrix competencies (e.g., Civic Knowledge, Ethical Decision-Making) are the specific, measurable sub-skills of the PoL's broad civic or critical thinking aspirations (e.g., "Responsible Citizen" or "Global Contributor"). You are providing the "how" for their agreed-upon "what." In essence, you are drilling down even more on the skills that are present in the PoL or PoG.

At the Department Level: A Coordinated Approach

The true transformative power happens when a department sits down together and works through the Matrix as a group. When a department works together to vertically align the standards and closes skill gaps, that is when you will see the greatest result.

BEST practices with collaboration: When we refer to the "department" or other collaborative groups, it is important to recognize the power of vertical and horizontal articulation with respect to ALL educators on the team. This includes special education teachers, teachers of MLs, teachers in the gifted programs, and other educational stakeholders. This type of articulation doesn't have to be isolated in terms of the standards but can also be within regular meetings with professional learning communities (PLCs) in which teachers discuss goals, analyze data, and brainstorm ideas together. Approaching this type of alignment work through the lens of a holistic view of authentic action civics may engage educators a bit more than if it is considered to be crossing off a requirement.

Perhaps it makes the most sense to design a Professional Development Goal together as a department and then work through it together, keeping each other accountable and allowing for a year long conversation about the goal. Below is a sample goal statement, focus area, and action steps aligned to the Matrix.

Sample Goal Statement: To establish the Portrait of a Citizen Matrix as the common language for curriculum and instruction within the Social Studies Department, ensuring vertical alignment and explicit scaffolding of all thirty civic skills by June (Table 10.2).

TABLE 10.2 Possible timeline to Portrait of a Citizen Integration

Timeline	*Focus Area*	*Action Steps Aligned to the Matrix*
By Sept.	Student engagement & baseline	Introduce the Portrait of a Citizen Matrix and the relevant "I Can" statements to students. Students complete a self-reflection (e.g., 1–5 rating scale) on the "I Can" statements to establish a baseline of perceived strengths and challenges and have department review results.
By Oct.	Departmental inventory & audit	Department uses the Matrix Staff Discovery Checklist to perform a current practice inventory. Identify "Hot Spots" (explicitly taught skills) and "Cold Spots" (curriculum gaps) within the department's collective curriculum map. Add specificity to lesson plans by explicitly naming the Matrix skill code (e.g., CT1) when it is implicitly addressed.
By Nov.	Vertical alignment planning	Hold a dedicated department meeting to discuss the "Hot Spots" identified in the audit. Begin drafting the Vertical Alignment Map for one competency…and draft the Shared Rubric for that competency, agreeing on the 4-point scale descriptions."
By Dec.	Systemic alignment & outreach	Overlay the Matrix skills with the existing Portrait of a Learner (PoL) competencies and the State Framework (leveraging generative AI for cross-referencing). Conduct an internal Rubric Calibration Session using past student work to fine-tune the drafted Shared Rubric before the implementation begins.

(*Continued*)

TABLE 10.2 (Continued)

Timeline	*Focus Area*	*Action Steps Aligned to the Matrix*
By Jan.	Action research cycle: Skill 1	Each department member selects one competency (e.g., Ethical Decision-Making). Choose Skill 1 within that competency. Design a lesson that explicitly teaches this skill using the "I Can" statement as the learning objective, and implement it.
By Feb.	Action research cycle: Skill 2 & Norming	Department meets to review student work from the January implementation, using the Shared Rubric (e.g., for Ethical Decision-Making) to norm scoring and ensure a consistent standard of rigor. Implement Skill 2 from the chosen competency in a new lesson.
By Mar.	Action research cycle: Skill 3	Implement Skill 3 from the chosen competency in a new lesson. Complete and finalize the Vertical Alignment Map for all 30 skills, identifying the primary teacher responsible for formal assessment of each skill.
By Apr.	Authentic assessment & reflection	Align an Authentic Learning Experience (e.g., an action civics project or policy brief) with the chosen competency, requiring students to apply all three implemented skills.
By May	Resource curation & growth reflection	Engage in a Common Planning Activity to gather, highlight, and categorize successful learning experiences that closely align with the focused competency (Resource Sharing). Have students complete a final self-reflection on the focused competency to measure their growth over the year (Growth Data).
By June	Roadmap & sustainability	Finalize the department's official Portrait of a Citizen Curriculum Roadmap (the completed Vertical Alignment Map). Set the second year's Professional Learning Goals focused on the next competency for the next school year, ensuring sustainability of the framework.

September and October: Introductions and An Honest Inventory

Of course you can start to integrate these skills at any time of the year, but if you are planning as a department to implement the Portrait of a Citizen Matrix, it always helps to start in September, when everyone is fresh and open to new ideas. This would be a good idea to introduce the "I Can" statements to your students and have them self-assess where they think they are in terms of each skill. Reviewing the language of the "I Can" statements will help as well so students know that they are active participants in their learning and acquisition of skills.

As a department, you need to have an honest inventory on current practices. This moves the Matrix from theoretical to a departmental tool. Each department member must determine what is already being taught, whether it is explicitly being taught or implicitly taught without the skills being named. The goal of discovery is not to change current lessons immediately, but to recognize that many Matrix skills are already implicit in quality social studies instruction. Teachers should start by reflecting on their best and most common assignments. With a Self-Audit Tool, you can provide a simple checklist of the 30 Matrix skills and ask your department to determine:

- **I Already Do This (Explicitly):** I use this skill's language, and it is assessed.
- **I Already Do This (Implicitly):** I teach this skill, but I don't name or assess it.
- **I Don't Do This:** This skill is currently absent from my course.

This phase validates your department's current expertise and shows that the Matrix is a way to refine and name their existing rigor, not replace it. Note that honesty about things that are not represented in current practice should not be met with feelings of inadequacy; rather, this is a way to guide for next steps and the Matrix is a means of communication.

> **BEST practices for all your students:** This is the time to also do an honest reflection and inventory of exactly who your students are. What are their backgrounds, cultures, languages, interests, and strengths? Use this information to guide you and to help you ensure that you are teaching culturally relevant and responsive content and pedagogy.

Matrix Staff Discovery Checklist

Instructions: For each of the 30 skills in the Portrait of a Citizen Matrix, mark the column that best describes its status in your current course curriculum (Table 10.3).

TABLE 10.3 Matrix Discovery Checklist

I Already Do This (Explicitly): I teach this skill, I use the "I Can" statement, and it is a formal component of assessment (e.g., on a rubric)	I Already Do This (Implicitly): I teach this skill, but I do not name the skill, use the "I Can" statement, or formally assess it.		I Don't Do This (Gap): This skill is currently absent from my course curriculum and is not taught.	
#	Skill description	**I Already Do This (Explicitly):** I teach this skill, I use the "I Can" statement, and it is a **formal component** of assessment (e.g., on a rubric).	**I Already Do This (Implicitly):** I teach this skill, but I do **not** name the skill, use the "I Can" statement, or formally assess it.	**I Don't Do This (Gap):** This skill is currently **absent** from my course curriculum and is not taught.
CK1	Foundational knowledge of government and civics			
CK2	Source evaluation and use (historical and civic)			
CK3	Civic systems knowledge (local, state, national)			
CK4	Interconnectedness of international organizations			

(*Continued*)

TABLE 10.3 (Continued)

CK5	Historical causation and context
EDM1	Value recognition and prioritization
EDM2	Analysis of ethical dilemmas
EDM3	Ethical dilemma resolution (Applying principles)
EDM4	Reflection on personal values and biases
EDM5	Understanding rights and responsibilities
CT1	Information analysis and evaluation
CT2	Perspective taking and empathy
CT3	Inquiry and research skill development
CT4	Conflict of interest identification
CT5	Problem definition and framing
EC1	Community needs assessment
EC2	Action planning and implementation
EC3	Collaboration and consensus-building
EC4	Advocacy and civic leadership
EC5	Reflective practice and adaptation

(Continued)

TABLE 10.3 (Continued)

DI1	Recognition of diverse identities and experiences
DI2	Understanding structural inequality and equity
DI3	Promotion of inclusive environments
DI4	Intercultural communication
DI5	Addressing historical injustice and reconciliation
DC1	Understanding political processes and participation
DC2	Active listening and dialogue
DC3	Argumentation and debate
DC4	Media and civic literacy
DC5	Civic engagement and voting

Departments can use the Matrix Checklist to identify "Hot Spots" (meaning explicitly taught skills) and "Cold Spots" (meaning curriculum gaps). Having each person identify their Hot and Cold Spots can lead to a great conversation on the Matrix, skills, and goals of the department.

The Goal is Rich Conversations that Create Substantive Change. When teachers arrive at the meeting with the audit completed, they can discuss where they address the skills, and where the gaps are. The key is to see if there is one area that has gaps across the board. The discussion around an audit can take quite a while, but can truly be some of the richest conversations you and your colleagues can have. You also can ask them to bring in 3–5 of their common unit plans or summative assessments and have colleagues identify which matrix skills are required to successfully complete those tasks. This will largely depend on your time. For example, if you have an hour of common planning time, this can happen over a number of those common times. If, however, you are given a half-day or full day of Professional Development just to vertically align and coordinate curriculum, this can be a very fruitful endeavor.

November and December: Developing Norms

These months are dedicated to drafting the Vertical Alignment Map. The work here is to collectively answer: "Who owns the introduction of this skill, and who owns the formal assessment of mastery?" The December step also ensures the Matrix aligns with the existing Portrait of a Learner (PoL), showing administrators that you are executing *their* vision. You can hold a dedicated department meeting to draft the Vertical Alignment Map for each competency, establishing the grade level responsible for Introduction, Reinforcement, and Formal Assessment for each skill within each competency.

Then take the Matrix and overlay it with your district's goals or Portrait of a Learner/Graduate, as well as the State Frameworks for social studies or civics. Remember, leveraging AI is helpful here for cross-referencing.

This may also be the time in which you intentionally and authentically reflect on how your current students will have access to the various activities, competencies, and skills. What are the strengths of the students in your classes this year and where may they need scaffolding? Working alongside your colleagues is important in all steps—but particularly here.

January, February, March: Intentional Implementation

The department takes on an intentional implementation, transitioning from planning to practice.

January: The Action Research Cycle: Starting in January, department members select one competency and one skill to focus on each month. This means dedicating January, February, and March to Skills 1, 2, and 3 within the chosen competency (e.g., Ethical Decision-Making). By focusing on only three skills, teachers can execute small, manageable changes in their lessons, which is crucial for preventing burnout.

February Norming Session: Teachers bring their lesson and the corresponding student work from January's implementation. The department then completes the process of norming, where you use the Shared Rubric (developed in November/December) to standardize expectations. This ensures that a "Proficient" score in 9th grade complies with the same level of rigor as a "Proficient" score in 12th grade.

March Alignment Check: In March, in addition to discussing the third skill implementation, you may need to re-visit and finalize the Vertical Alignment Map for all 30 skills. This is the moment to adjust ownership based on any challenges identified during the norming process.

April and May: Synthesis and Evidence

These months focus on using the Matrix for authentic assessment and data collection.

April: Stacking Skills into Authentic Assessment: The department highlights successful learning experiences that align with the focused competency. Students apply the three new, stacked skills in a culminating project (e.g., an action civics brief or policy recommendation). This demonstrates that the skills transfer into a real-world context.

May: Growth Data and Reflection: Students use the "I Can" statements to reflect on their final growth. This generates the necessary Growth Data for department review. Compare the data to the first survey in September to see how students have grown, providing a powerful, data-driven narrative about the success of the year-long Professional Learning Goal.

June: Developing the Roadmap for the Next Year

In June, you will have the benefit of a year's worth of experiences, a Vertical Alignment Map, and surveys from students to determine how successful you have been with implementation of the Matrix. As a department it will be time to decide how you will ensure sustainability of the framework.

Making the Matrix Your Own: The Power of Local Adaptation

While the Portrait of a Citizen Matrix provides a robust foundation of 30 universal civic skills, no single framework can perfectly hit all the notes for every unique school community. Your school, your department, and your community's ethos—its values, language, and priorities—must be the ultimate guide. The Matrix is not set in stone. It is designed to be flexible, encouraging you to make the information work for you. You are empowered to adjust this framework to meet your specific needs. You know your district—and your students—best.

At the District Level

Communicating the Matrix to Caregivers and Stakeholders

Communicating the Matrix externally is essential for building support and ensuring transparency. The most effective strategies are those that integrate the Matrix into existing workflows, allowing teachers to share valuable, specific feedback without adding excessive time or effort.

Consider introducing the Matrix as part of your back to school night, highlighting the skills that will be learned and strengthened rather than the grades that students will receive. It's a good idea to align the Matrix with the school priorities or the Portrait of a Learner/Graduate so parents can easily see how the Matrix fits in with what they already know about benchmarks of the school.

Learning Management System

You can consider posting the Matrix on your Learning Management System like Google Classroom, and using it as a guide for lessons. Parents have the option to be a part of the classrooms, so they will be able to reference back to the skills referenced in the lessons. It will also help if you use the language of the Matrix in your rubrics along with your lessons, units and projects.

Conferences and Grades

Using the language of the Matrix in your grades and grading will help foster transparency between you, your student, and their caregivers. During conference time and other meetings, have the Matrix on hand to ensure that you are all on the same page as you are discussing the student's progress.

Seal of Civic Readiness

Civic Education is what students learn. Civic Engagement is what students do. Civic Outcomes are what students become (Rogers Bascom & Pinkham, 2025, Slide 14). How does one measure that outcome? One way might be creating a Seal of Civic Readiness. The National Council for Social Studies (n.d.) has created a toolkit for creating a path promoting and encouraging civic participation called the "Seal of Civic Readiness." This would mirror the state Seals of Biliteracy, supplemental endorsements on a high school diploma that state a student has gone above and beyond the normal course of learning to achieve a higher mark than his or her peers. At the time of this writing, five states (New York, California, Georgia, Virginia, and Arizona) have created benchmarks for students to achieve in the areas of civic knowledge, community participation, and service. The Seal of Civic Readiness would be an excellent way to showcase the learning that has taken place as a result of the implementation of the Portrait of a Citizen Matrix. It would be even more powerful if you included students in the creation of the requirements and measurement of outcomes. Look for timelines, letters of advocacy, and state examples on the NCSS website.

Conclusion: The Hope for Our Students

We want our students to be informed, active, and enthusiastic citizens. Moving from theoretical to actual is challenging yet satisfying. Your work delivers on the central promise of the Portrait of a Citizen Matrix. This framework is not an accident—it's a curriculum built on step-by-step, stackable skills that help our students become active participants in their democracy. You have moved past isolated lessons and established a coherent, vertically-aligned system. The true hope for our students lies in the intentionality you have created by wrestling with the Matrix and making it work for you and your department.

This intentionality is the guarantee that when students graduate, they will possess durable, transferable skills *and civic knowledge* to navigate a complex and polarized world. It is the confidence to know that they have been consistently taught to be active contributors in their communities. By establishing clear competencies and a rigorous process for assessment, you have solidified the core civic purpose of your curriculum. Remember, the Matrix is flexible; its strength is in its capacity to adapt to your school's ethos, ensuring it is a living document that serves the unique needs of your students.

This framework is what separates a hopeful wish for democracy from a genuine, coherent instructional plan to sustain it. You have built the pathway and committed to the process. You have the blueprint, the shared language, and the team. Now, continue to walk the path with dedication. The future of the civic landscape depends on the sustained rigor and resolve you bring to the classroom every single day.

References

National Council for the Social Studies. (n.d.). *NCSS seal of civic readiness toolkit*. https://www.socialstudies.org/advocacy/ncss-seal-civic-readiness-toolkit

Rogers Bascom, J., & Pinkham, R. (2025, December 6). *Empowering youth: Achieving the state seal of civic engagement through service learning* [SLide show]. Retrieved from https://docs.google.com/presentation/d/1Qm691uR4C_0C8VY2BdCgFSmeTKTjXVLikR0pBnjzUiQ/edit

11

Conclusion

The Call to Action

What does success look like? It could look like a recent graduate and registered voter, who doesn't wait to be told what to do, but is already engaged. It could look like a young adult who, upon encountering a complex local issue, immediately researches its historical and global context. They should be able to instinctively filter the news for bias and propaganda before possibly hosting a community meeting where they listen deeply to different viewpoints, especially those they disagree with. They may be people who do local advocacy on behalf of others or engage in their community in a positive way. In fact, they may not be documented citizens, but they take on the role of valued contributors to our society and our activism. This graduate could possibly facilitate a discussion that seeks not just consensus, but an ethical, compromise-driven solution, and then maybe mobilize a diverse team to implement that change. This is the Portrait of a Citizen in action, and it is the only way to ensure our students graduate as participants and not merely residents.

Does it have to be this perfect to be a success? Absolutely not. What if a student walks out with most of these attributes? Would that be enough? Maybe they are an introvert and won't be leading any discussions anytime soon, but would they be willing to participate in the discussion? Would they be able to

DOI: 10.4324/9781003746614-11

see the discussion for what it is? Would they listen with an open mind? Maybe they won't be hosting a community meeting, but would they be more likely to attend one? Would they be more willing to lend their voice when they see injustice? Would they be more likely to vote? The essential factor is that they have the skills to move forward as an engaged citizen, and the confidence to employ those skills. Those skills are carefully built upon each other, stacking knowledge and knowhow in a way that builds confidence and security.

The Work Begins Now

That possibility of an engaged citizen as a high school graduate is the driving force behind this entire framework. Throughout this book, we've explored a profound and urgent crisis: the marginalization of civic education, the atrophy of civil discourse, and the resulting decline in active, informed engagement across our communities. We began with the stark reality—that less than one in four 8th graders demonstrates proficiency in civics—and we acknowledged the deep challenge facing every educator: how do we prepare students to navigate a world defined by division and misinformation?

The answer, we found, is not in adding more content, but in mastering essential **skills**. We can't simply *hope* that students will transition from passive observers to active participants; we must intentionally design the curriculum to build that crucial bridge and make sure our students build those skills like an athlete builds muscle, a little at a time, getting stronger and stronger as they go. It can't wait; the best time to start is now.

The Blueprint for a Citizen, or a Civic Participant

The **Portrait of a Citizen Matrix** is more than just a framework; it is the blueprint for intentionally building those skills. It moves the abstract goal of "good citizenship" into a tangible, measurable language that we can teach, assess, and replicate. This

Matrix, built upon the familiar structure of a Portrait of a Learner, defines six core competencies that guarantee civic readiness:

- **Civic Knowledge:** *The foundational understanding of how our government and history function* is critical for citizens to understand as we empower ourselves as contributing and participatory members of society.
- **Community Engagement:** *The willingness to take informed action beyond the classroom walls and connect with the community around them* defines the ways that citizens can make a difference at a local level and shows us the importance of local civil engagement.
- **Ethical Decision-Making:** *The ability to navigate competing values, seek compromise, and act with integrity* guides citizens in seeing the larger picture of issues and understanding how we consider the ways to view them through a lens of empathy and justice.
- **Critical Thinking:** *The skill set required to identify bias, reject propaganda, and rely on evidence, to be skeptical and to question motivations* prepares us to seek answers beyond the surface and engage in research that provides us with facts to guide our viewpoints and actions.
- **National and Global Awareness:** *The recognition of the complex, interconnected systems shaping their world* opens our eyes to life beyond our immediate area and understanding to see the interconnectedness of the various countries and cultures around the world.
- **Differences Celebrated:** *The commitment to respectful discourse, active listening, and leveraging diverse perspectives to strengthen democracy* helps us recognize that differences are not bad or harmful to our ways of life and that we want to learn from diverse perspectives to grow as humans.

By adopting the "I Can" statements associated with these competencies, you are providing your students—and your department—with a common, clear language for success and ownership of our actions. You are making the implicit explicit, ensuring that no student graduates without the tools necessary to have a voice.

The Synthesis: From Knowing to Doing

When we look at these six skills as a whole, we see a path, grouping them into three distinct, mutually reinforcing stages of civic practice. The first is The Stage of Foundation, which builds the intellectual scaffolding: *what do I need to know* (Civic Knowledge) and *what is the scope* of my responsibility (National and Global Awareness)?

This foundation then feeds into The Stage of Analysis, focusing on processing the world around us with intellectual rigor. Here, the student determines: *How do I weigh* my values and principles (Ethical Decision-Making), and *how do I discern* truth and evaluate sources (Critical Thinking)?

Finally, the learning becomes visible in The Stage of Application, where students interact directly with the world. This is the practical test: *How do I mobilize* with others to solve a tangible problem (Community Engagement), and *how do I ensure* that my actions are inclusive and respectful of those I disagree with (Differences Celebrated)? The true Citizen is the one who fluidly moves between these stages, proving that democracy is a verb, not a noun.

These are the building blocks to set our students up for success, not just in the work world (where these skills are also incredibly important) but in the civic world. We were not just meant to work, we were meant to create, to question, and to thrive. That's what we want for our students, and our own children.

The Educator's Role: The Essential Work

This is democratic renewal, and you are on the front lines. We know that teaching the stackable skills of citizenship is perhaps the most challenging and essential work in education today. Your classroom is a vital refuge for critical analysis, open inquiry, and the respectful celebration of differences.

The Matrix empowers you to make your already excellent teaching to connect historical context to present-day action, and theoretical knowledge to real-world consequences. It is through your *intentional* guidance, your willingness to tackle controversial issues safely, and your commitment to accessibility (through BEST practices) that this generation will learn that being a "good citizen" means not just following rules, but having the courage to question and advocate for what is right and to recognize it's the differences that make us stronger.

This is not easy work. It is the long game. But by planting the seeds of civic competence today, we assure a future where the people are enlightened, engaged, and capable of sustaining the self-governance we cherish. The best time to plant a tree was twenty years ago. The second best time is now.

Thank you for doing the essential work! You are shaping the leaders of both today and tomorrow, and the citizens who will take our country forward using the skills they learned with you.

John Lewis (2012) wrote,

> Take a long, hard look down the road you will have to travel once you have made a commitment to work for change. Know that this transformation will not happen right away. Change often takes time. It rarely happens all at once.

Reference

Lewis, J. (2012). *Across that bridge: A vision for change and the future of America*. Hachette Books.

For Product Safety Concerns and Information please contact our EU representative GPSR@taylorandfrancis.com Taylor & Francis Verlag GmbH, Kaufingerstraße 24, 80331 München, Germany

Batch number: 10476193

Printed by Printforce, the Netherlands